Interdisciplinary Unit
Growth & Change
CHALLENGING

Illustrator:
Agi Palinay

Editor:
Walter Kelly, M.A.

Editorial Project Manager:
Ina Massler Levin, M.A.

Editor-in-Chief:
Sharon Coan, M.S. Ed.

Cover Artist:
Sue Fullam

Art Director:
Elayne Roberts

Product Manager:
Phil Garcia

Imaging:
Hillary Merriman

Publishers:
Rachelle Cracchiolo, M.S. Ed.
Mary Dupuy Smith, M.S. Ed.

Author:
Evelyn Cole McNeilly, M.A., M.F.A.

Teacher Created Materials, Inc.
P.O. Box 1040
Huntington Beach, CA   92647
ISBN-1-55734-622-4

©1995 Teacher Created Materials, Inc.   Made in U.S.A.

Table of Contents

═══

Acknowledgements

Ideas and passages have been cited from the following works:

Forming, Thinking, Writing, The Composing Imagination by Ann Berthoff. Used by permission of Ann Berthoff and Heinemann Publications

Reading the Numbers by Mary Blocksma. Copyright (c) 1989 by Mary Blocksma. Used by permission of Viking Penguin, a division of Penguin Books USA, Inc.

The Power of Place by Winifred Gallagher. Copyright (c) 1993. Used by permission of Simon & Schuster, Inc.

Innumeracy, Mathematical Illiteracy and Its Consequences by John Allen Paulos. Copyright (c) 1988. Used by permission of Farrar, Straus & Giroux, Inc., Book Publishers division of Hill & Wang.

Creative Analysis by Albert Upton, Richard W. Samson, and Ann Dahlstrom Farmer. Used by permission of Richard W. Samson

Letters at 3 A.M. by Michael Ventura. Used by permission of Michael Ventura.

Mathematics Education for a Changing World by Stephen S. Willoughby. Used by permission of Stephen S. Willoughby.

Introduction

- ◆ Rocks and dunes form.

- ◆ Cells grow and divide.

- ◆ Plants and animals grow.

- ◆ Technology grows—in leaps.

- ◆ Corporations grow and often divide.

- ◆ Countries grow and change.

- ◆ Words grow and change in form and meaning.

- ◆ Artists grow, standing on the shoulders of each previous generation of artists.

- ◆ Musicians grow, standing on the shoulders of mathematicians, poets, and previous generations of musicians.

Intermediate students undergo dramatic bursts of growth, both physically and intellectually. Since schools are primarily concerned with the latter, educators are seeking better ways to meet that ever-expanding challenge.

Students between 11 and 13 years of age are just beginning to climb the "ladder of abstraction." They are at a stage of development that embraces concept formation. This unit is designed to help them recognize abstractions and "see" varying degrees of concretion in each subject in the curriculum.

These are the main goals of *Growth and Change:*

- ◆ To help students make connections within a course and from course to course

- ◆ To help students speed understanding

- ◆ To help students clarify thinking

- ◆ To empower students' minds to expand and grow in all areas

Designed to be taught simultaneously in all classes, this text works best at the beginning of the school year so its activities can be revisited throughout the year in any class, with any content. However, it can be adapted anytime and anywhere.

The Power of Abstraction

(Introduction for Teachers)

Intelligence is the ability to perceive relationships at high levels of abstraction.

—Albert Upton

1. A well-educated person is one who knows what he does not know.

2. Children realize there are many things they do not know.

3. Instill in them the habit of articulating what they do not know, and they will become well-educated.

4. To instill this habit, we show them how . . .

    ◆ to scamper up and down the abstraction ladder,

    ◆ to place known data in the pigeonholes of growing classification diagrams,

    ◆ to discover how parts relate to the whole and how stages in time relate to substages.

The Abstraction Ladder

Synthesize

(form concepts)

Analyze

(examine parts and their relationships)

Observe

(gather percepts)

All of our conscious experience—what happens that we are aware of—is made up of *sensation* (what we discover through our senses), *emotion* (physical, visceral responses), and the *logical perception* of similarity and difference which, in humans, becomes the *power of abstraction*.

Immanuel Kant (1724–1804) wrote, "Percepts without concepts are empty. Concepts without percepts are blind."

In other words, our perceptions—what we see, hear, feel, smell, and taste—are the sources of our daily intake of information. Through them we learn the rules of a given sport, how to construct a useful object out of wood, how to derive meaning from written text and other visual presentations, how to conduct scientific experiments, how to smell danger.

The Power of Abstraction *(cont.)*

Myriad perceptions by themselves are, in Kant's sense, empty. "What is the point?" you might ask when bombarded with facts. However, if the bombardier says, "The reasons for these details are . . ." or "Note how these details are similar to and relate to . . .," the perceptions are no longer empty facts. A concept ties them together, filling their veins with the blood of purpose.

Concepts alone are blind. Marx came up with the intriguing concept that all people could own and/or share material goods in common. The percepts that come from observing human behavior, however, do not support a Marxist system of government. The concept may be interesting, but the willingness of people to support it is missing. Therefore, the concept is blind.

To avoid the trap of empty percepts or blind concepts, we use the abstraction ladder. With it, we can visualize the relative generality or specificity of data.

The Power of Abstraction *(cont.)*

The Language of Science

In the language of the physical sciences, "Facts are the building blocks of science. These blocks are held together by theories, or ideas that explain groups of facts."

Theories operate at a relatively high level of abstraction, but they need low-level facts to support them. (Einstein perceived the relationship between space and time. To do so, he climbed many mathematical rungs on the ladder of abstraction.)

The scientific method involves going up and down the ladder. First, we observe low-level phenomena. Next, we analyze our observations by performing experiments to determine whether our observations are accurate. Third, we synthesize—that is, we put our observations together in new ways and climb the abstraction ladder to form a hypothesis that explains our observations. Finally, we go back down the ladder and test our hypothesis by checking our theory's prediction against new observations. Does what holds true in this case also hold true in all other cases?

The Language of Sports

In the language of sports, rules add tension to any game by providing the boundaries that players push against as they push against each other or as they challenge themselves. Examples that sit on the lower rungs of the abstraction ladder:

- You cannot go across the line of scrimmage in football until after the ball is snapped.

- You cannot try to hit the pitched ball in baseball after three strikes.

- You cannot move the golf ball when it is in play.

All these specific conditions fall under the abstraction of rules.

The Language of Art

In the language of art we begin with photographic representations of objects, animals, and people. As the artist thinks about the concept he is trying to convey, he distorts photographic representation. At midpoint on an artist's ladder the viewer can recognize the percept. At the top of the ladder the viewer may see two colors on a canvas and nothing more. If the viewer has followed the growth and development of art throughout its history, he understands the concept and "feels" the communication. If the viewer is not familiar with the history of art, he may say, "Any kindergarten kid could do that." In other words, since he does not see the roots, he may not feel the power of the abstraction.

The Power of Abstraction *(cont.)*

The Language of Composition

(1) In the language of composition, we ask students to look for "cohesiveness" in each other's writing. (2) The abstraction ladder helps us explain that in cohesive writing the degree of specificity of a given sentence is very close to the sentences that surround it. (3) In other words, the writer climbs or descends the abstraction ladder rung by rung. (4) He does not skip rungs.

Note each sentence above. They are numbered in order of descent on the ladder, number one being the most abstract or general, and number four the most concrete or specific.

The Language of Literature

In the language of literature we speak of the "depth" of one author's work, the "shallowness" of another. Obviously, we need a longer ladder to climb into and out of a deep hole than we need for a shallow one.

The Language of Mathematics

In the language of mathematics, problem solving is at the top of the ladder, estimating not far below, and general use of a calculator below estimating. Wouldn't such specific functions as addition, multiplication, and division fall on the lowest rungs? Where would geometry fall?

Geometric figures are like much of Picasso's art, recognizable as representative of something we have seen on earth but obviously not photographic representation.

Actually, geometry and physics are co-dependent. When you hammer a nail, the angle of the nail (geometry) determines the effect of the attempted penetration (physics).

A Venn diagram, like the abstraction ladder, is used to solve problems. Both help us visualize relationships.

The Language of Social Studies

In the language of social studies, the question "Are social systems progressing or simply changing?" would be high up the ladder. The statement "The predominant religion of the people of England is Protestant because Henry the VIII wanted a divorce and the rules of Catholicism forbade divorce" would be midway on the ladder. The statement "Vasco de Gama, Renaissance explorer from Portugal, was the first person to go to Asia by sailing around Africa to India," would sit comfortably on a lower rung. It would take a long ladder with several rungs to connect the three statements under the higher abstraction level of human curiosity. However, it can be done.

Each discipline is an approach to ordering the world and our experience in it. None has a complete answer, all need each other, and all live comfortably with partial theory.

Classroom Management

The student exercises in this chapter demonstrate the use of the abstraction ladder, as well as the three kinds of analysis. (Answer keys appear on pages 202–208.) The student tasks lend themselves more to portfolio assessment than letter grades, although both can be used. Scoring rubrics for writing assignments are included for each prompt for student use. Because most of the lessons are designed for small group work (five to six students), below are some suggestions for classroom management of small groups.

(Since each teacher, to survive, must exercise control over his class, and since each teacher's mode of control matches his/her personality, the following suggestions may not work for everyone. However, they have been tested extensively and do work well for most.)

1. Tell students that in the adult world of work we rarely have the chance to choose with whom we work. Instead of suffering the stress of personality clashes, we learn to work around our differences by following specific rules and accentuating our common goals.

2. Arbitrarily select group members, either by counting 1, 2, 3, 4, 5 and seating all the like numbers together or by having students pick numbers or colors from a hat. Strips of colored construction paper distributed by classroom rows will group the students and provide immediate names for each group—by color.

3. Assign roles to students in each group or let them work out who does what. Roles may be those of Spokesperson, Recorder, Timekeeper, Mollifier, and Taskmaster. (Other titles, of course, may be used in place of these suggested ones.)

4. Determine individual talents of group members. If every member of the group knows that one of its members goes skiing often, they know who to turn to when a question arises relating to that sport. If each member knows that one of them works the local swap meet regularly, they know who to turn to in related matters. It is imperative that the group as a whole knows all of its resources.

Classroom Management *(cont.)*

Since most students see themselves as having no special talents, it takes some structured digging to bring out each student's field of expertise. Peer pressure can be an ally here, as can a brief questionnaire that jogs the students' minds and gives them permission to brag a little.

> 5. Finally, the power of whatever assessment tool you are using can motivate cooperative behavior. Establish criteria for group evaluations. Those students who sabotage the group should feel immediate consequences (best in the form of exclusion) coupled with private counsel. Part of each student's assessment portfolio can be teacher judgment regarding group behavior. Here is a suggested checklist:
>   1. Student listens as much as he/she speaks.
>   2. Student takes responsibility for the group.
>   3. Student speaks as much as he/she listens.
>   4. Student maintains focus on task at hand.
>   5. Student values courtesy.

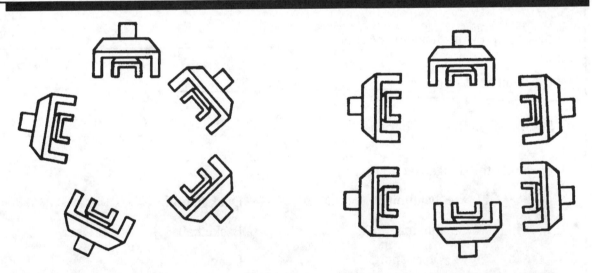

Once the groups are established, the exercises in this text will help cement them into smoothly functioning entities. When new students enter a class, the teacher needs to place them in appropriate groups. It is important to allow at least a week for them to assimilate, and it helps to have a specific procedure. Following (page 10) is a suggested questionnaire to be used at initial group formation and for entering new students.

So that students understand that they must know how to read in all sources, each section contains some interesting selections that may be used as reading lessons. Have students underline any words they do not understand and make notes—comments or questions in the section to the right of the text. If you think the reading level is too difficult for your students, you may want to read some of them aloud. Upon completion of the reading, have students write, using the prompts at the end of this section or one of your choosing. Prompts include scoring guides for student and teacher use.

The following pages are reproducible for student use.

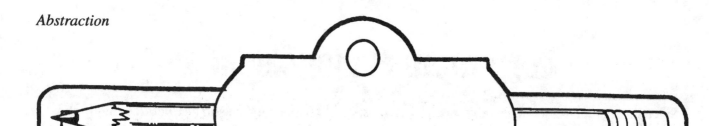

Questionnaire for Group Work

1. Your full name: _____

2. The name you want others to use when speaking to you: _____

3. Your favorite music or musicians: _____

4. Your favorite foods: _____

5. Your previous hometown/school: _____

6. Number of brothers: _____ sisters:_____

7. Your favorite TV programs:_____

8. Circle the things you do best:

   - Swimming
   - Singing
   - Other sport
   - Telling stories
   - Brainstorming
   - Skiing
   - Soccer
   - Writing
   - Making others laugh

   - Duck hunting
   - Basketball
   - Dancing
   - Building things
   - Needlework
   - Drawing pictures
   - Helping others
   - Fixing broken things
   - Crafts

Name _____ Date _____

The Abstraction Ladder

All of our conscious experience—what happens that we are aware of—is made up of *sensation* (what we discover through our senses), *emotion* (physical, visceral responses), and the *logical recognition* of how things are alike and how they are different. This recognition, or perception, in humans becomes the power of *abstraction*.

On the lines below, explain how an ant is like an oak tree.

To answer above, you had to "climb the imaginary abstraction ladder" for both the ant and the oak before you could "see" how they are alike.

Name _____ Date _____

The Abstraction Ladder *(cont.)*

At the foot of the abstraction ladder is the concrete thing we can see, hear, touch, smell, name, and put into some sort of general classification that is up on a higher rung of the ladder. A poodle is a dog, is a canine, is an animal. A woman is a human, is a Homo Sapiens, is an animal. Both, like the ant and the oak tree, grow. They are alive.

On which rung of the ladder would you place the ability to move from place to place? Above or below alive?

(Discuss your reasoning in your group then write your individual answer below.)

Why?_____

_____

_____

_____

_____

_____

_____

_____

_____

_____

_____

_____

Levels of Abstraction

It is easy to see how people are different from one another. It takes climbing the abstraction ladder to see how they are alike.

The level of abstraction, or generalization, is the relative degree to which things are similar and different. You probably have already noticed that the similarities among ants far outnumber the differences. The opposite occurs when we compare an ant with an oak tree. The word *ant* operates at a low level of abstraction. The word *organism* operates at a high level. *Hen, chicken, fowl,* and *animal* operate at various levels of abstraction. Things named at low levels of abstraction have many qualities in common, and things named at high levels of abstraction have few qualities in common.

Name _____ Date _____

The Abstraction Ladder *(cont.)*

Try This

On the left side of the page below, make a quick list of 10 things you see in the room. (You may take five minutes.) Next, sort them by qualities they have in common—for example, writing instruments. Then place the names of each thing or group of things on an appropriate rung of the ladder on the right side below. Swap finished ladders with the others in your group. Discuss any differences you might suggest in the ladders. Try to explain and understand the reasons for any changes.

1. _____

2. _____

3. _____

4. _____

5. _____

6. _____

7. _____

8. _____

9. _____

10. _____

(Abstract)

(Concrete)

Memory Aid

The normal human brain can recall seven isolated bits of stored data with ease. Beyond seven, it's a struggle involving rote memorization. If, however, we memorize seven categories with seven items in each category, we can easily recall 49 items. The key to easy recall fits in the doors of analysis.

Name _____ Date _____

Analysis

Question: How are language and mathematics alike?

Answer: They are both abstract systems of symbols (invented by humans) which stand for concrete things. They are tools to help us make order out of chaos. (How do you put your room in order when your mother calls it a "chaotic mess"?)

To create, we take concrete things or their symbols apart and put them together in new ways.

- ◆ Taking apart is called *analysis.*
- ◆ Putting together is called *synthesis.*

We begin with analysis. There are three kinds: *classification, structure,* and *operation.*

To classify things, we answer these questions: "What is this a sort of?" and "What are the sorts of this?"

To perform a structure analysis, we answer these questions: "What is this a part of?" and "What are the parts of this?"

And when we do an operation analysis, we answer these questions: "What is this a stage of?" and "What are the stages of this?"

When we say, "A person is a sort of animal," we are classifying. When we say, "A hand is a part of a person," we are doing a structure analysis. When we say, "Adolescence is a stage of a person's life," we are making an operation analysis.

- ◆ Classification has to do with *kinds of things.*
- ◆ Structure analysis has to do with *parts of things.*
- ◆ Operation analysis has to do with *stages of change in things.*

In your group, write two examples of each kind of analysis.

Classification

_____

_____

Structure

_____

_____

Operation

_____

_____

Classification Analysis

(from *Creative Analysis* by Albert Upton, Richard W. Samson, and Ann Dahlstrom Farmer, page 63)

The major terms for classification analysis follow:

- ◆ **genus**
- ◆ **species**
- ◆ **specimen**
- ◆ **quality**
- ◆ **vertical sorting factor**
- ◆ **horizontal sorting factor**

1. The terms *genus* and *species* used in classification are logical rather than biological. (Logical is more abstract than biological because the *bio* prefix limits its meaning.)

2. In classification analysis, a genus is simply the name of a class, and species terms are the names of the two or more subclasses the genus includes.

3. Genus and species appear above *vertical lines*, implying that the terms below are similar.

4. *Horizontal lines* represent the two or more species that differ.

5. An individual of a species is called a *specimen*.

6. To determine placement on any given abstraction ladder or classification diagram, we must perceive or "see" similarities and differences.

7. To see how things are alike or different, we separate the thing from its qualities.

8. Qualities are abstract because our minds abstract (or *detach*) them from the things that have them. The color "blue" is a quality that many things have in common. The following will illustrate this idea:

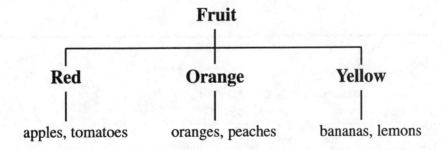

The sorting factor here is *color*. The fruits would be classified in a different way if we were concerned with the quality of *taste, texture,* or *shape*.

Name _____ Date _____

Classification Analysis *(cont.)*

(For the following task each group of students needs a deck of cards that are copies of the animals pictured on page 17.)

1. Look at all of the cards in your stack.

2. Write a name for the entire stack.

3. What qualities do the things have in common?

4. What are the differences?

5. Make a diagram. At the end of each vertical line, make a horizontal line to represent the quality by which the specimens below it differ.

6. Label the divisions (the sample diagram below shows two) and then place your cards in the proper division.

Animals

Classification Analysis *(cont.)*

A B C D

E F G H

I J K L

M N O P

Q R S T

Name _____ Date _____

Classification Analysis *(cont.)*

There are two sorts of classification: classifications of collected specimens (such as your cards of animal pictures) and classifications of specimens to be collected. The latter is called a *working classification*. It is much like a grocery list when the items you want to buy are classified by type or by placement in the store.

A working classification is a statement of intention; it points out possibilities that may not occur to us if we limit our attention to specimens we can see.

Now, look at your stack of cards. Suppose your intention is to order food for the animals. Fill in the pigeonholes in the classification diagram below with the corresponding letters on your cards.

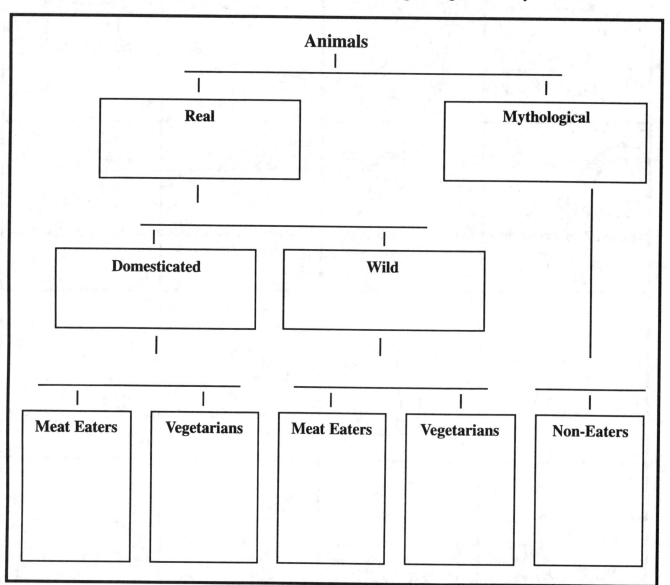

Note differences in the diagram from your original. Now turn over your paper and list as many animals as you can from memory.

Name _____ Date _____

Classification Analysis *(cont.)*

Analyze the objects pictured below so that you can name them from memory. Make a classification diagram first. If you wish, you may use the hints for grouping that appear to the sides of the objects.

Useful Objects Classification Diagram

Name _____ Date _____

Classification Analysis *(cont.)*

Make a working classification of automobiles. Use at least four vertical sorting factors—for example, *electric-powered* might be one.

Automobiles

Name _____ Date _____

Classification Analysis *(cont.)*

Make a list of all the subjects you are currently taking in school:

1. _____   5. _____

2. _____   6. _____

3. _____   7. _____

4. _____   8. _____

In your group, discuss the things you learn in each subject. Have one person record your ideas by subject. Answer these questions: How are the subjects alike? How many horizontal sorting factors do you have? What are they?

Draw your classification diagram below. Fill in the pigeonholes with the numbers that correspond with subjects you listed above. (Teacher's key has a sample diagram.)

Compare your diagram with those in other groups. Reach consensus as a class on your horizontal sorting factors.

Structure Analysis

(from *Creative Analysis*, page 76)

The major terms of structure analysis are these:

- **part**
- **whole**
- **joint**
- **anatomizing factor**

The words *part* and *whole* signify the relationship of their inclusion in space. In certain cases things which are normally considered parts may be thought of as wholes. A hand may be called a whole if we are concerned with its parts. In structure analysis the largest thing we are concerned with is called a *whole.* Thus, the classroom is a whole classroom, but it is also part of the school, and the school is part of the school district.

A *joint* is a connection between two or more parts. The wall between two classrooms is a joint—in this sense of the word. A joint is any point, line, surface, or space between adjoining parts. Joints may be actual or projected, as in a blueprint.

An *anatomizing factor* is the name of a joint or class of joints. Anatomizing factors point out the places where structures are divided into parts. Thus, such words as *corner, line, edge, connection, plane, middle, side,* and *boundary* stand for a whole class of joints.

Analyze the structure below and the diagram on the next page so you can reproduce it from memory on a separate sheet of paper.

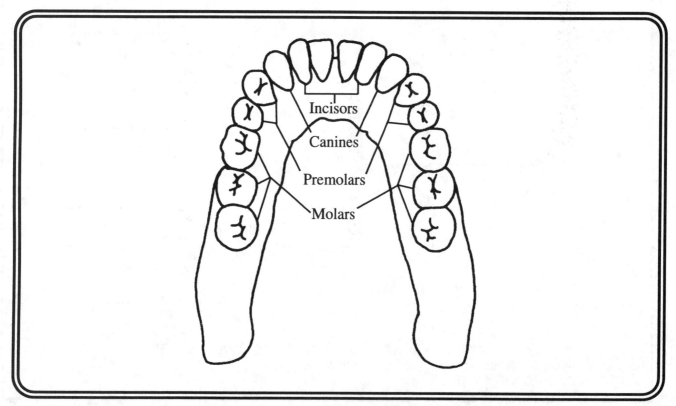

Structure Analysis *(cont.)*

Name _____ Date _____

Finish this structure analysis diagram of teeth.

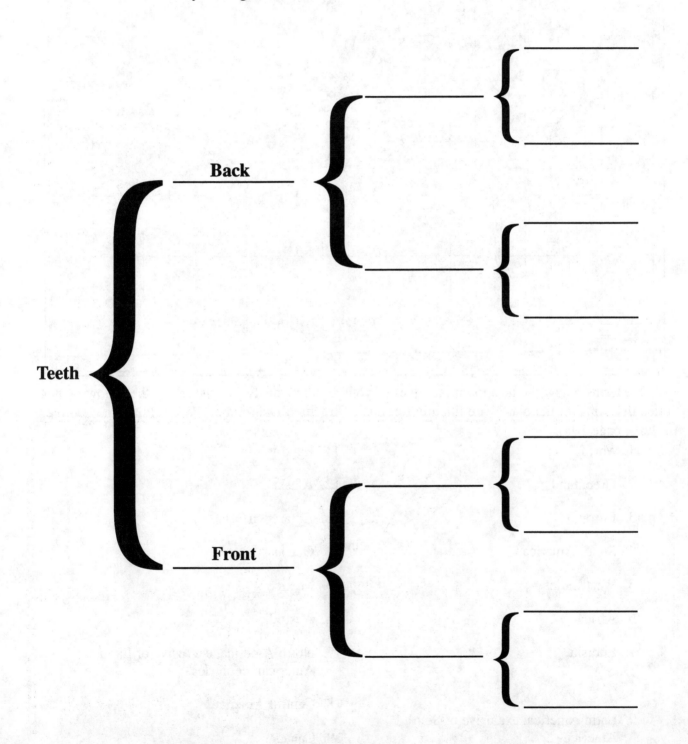

Now turn this page over and list the teeth from memory.

Structure Analysis (cont.)

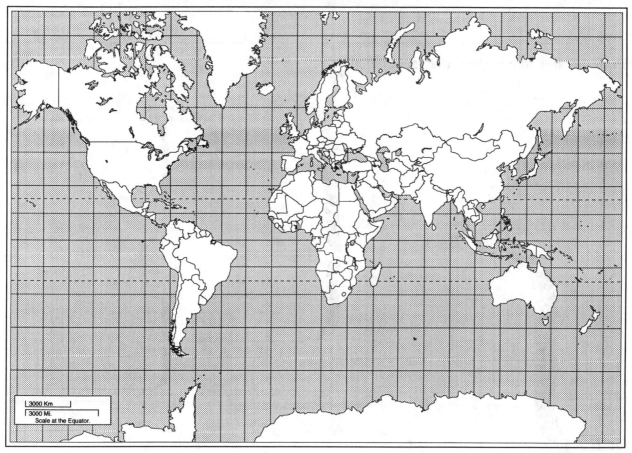

Place the terms below on the appropriate lines of your structure analysis diagram on the following page. Notice that some of the blanks are filled in for you. (Structural Diagram of the World, from *Creative Analysis*, page 106)

1. World

2. Greenland

3. Europe

4. South America

5. West Indies

6. Africa

7. Eurasia

8. Asia

9. Latin America, exclusive of South America

10. United States, exclusive of Alaska

11. Land

12. Alaska

13. Antarctica

14. Ocean

15. Mexico

16. Australia

17. North America, exclusive of Latin American countries

18. Central America

19. Canada

20. North America

Name _____ Date _____

Structure Analysis *(cont.)*

Structure Diagram

Please note the fundamental difference and fundamental similarity between classification and structure analysis. Just as there are no joints in the one, so there are no pigeonholes in the other. The name of a classification is the name of all the pigeonholes, full or empty. The name of a structure analysis is the name of the entire structure.

After you have completed the diagram, study it, turn the page over, and see how many parts of the structure you can recall.

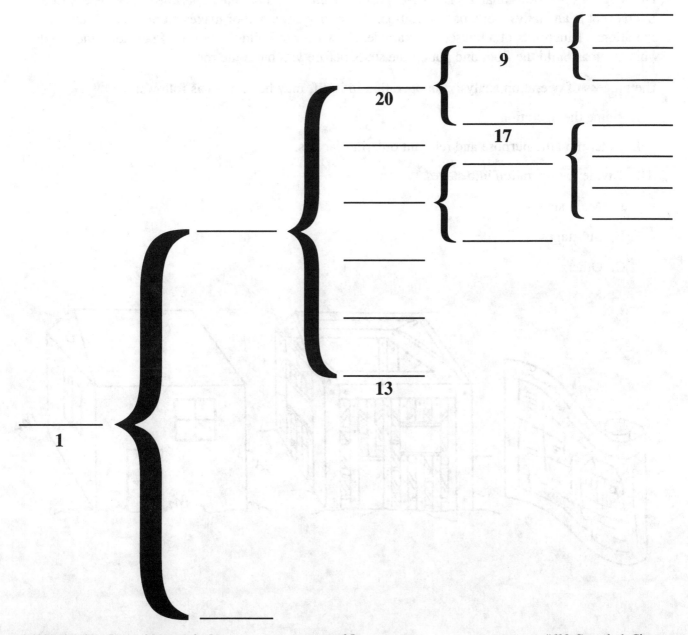

Operation Analysis

(from *Creative Analysis,* pages 90-92)

The major terms of operation analysis are these:

◆ stage ◆ operation ◆ juncture ◆ ordering factor ◆ purpose

An *operation* is a structure changing in time and space for a purpose. A *stage* is a temporal unit (a segment of time) of an operation. For instance, a basketball game is an operation consisting of stages such as the first quarter and second quarter which make up the first half. Operation analysis is the process of dividing operations into their temporal units. The process is determined by the *purpose*.

Junctures are points of division between stages, just as joints are places of division between parts in structure analysis.

Two sorts of operations analysis are these: *past operations* and *planned operations*. A history of a given event is an analysis of a past operation. A builder or an author makes an outline of planned operations. Blueprints of a house, for example, show how to build the house. Plans tell when to do what, such as build the floor and put up the studs before you build the roof.

The process of operation analysis, an operation in itself, may be divided as follows:

  I. Name the operation.

 II. Determine the purpose and relevant ordering factors.

III. Divide the operation into stages.

   A. Main stages

   B. Substages

   C. Others

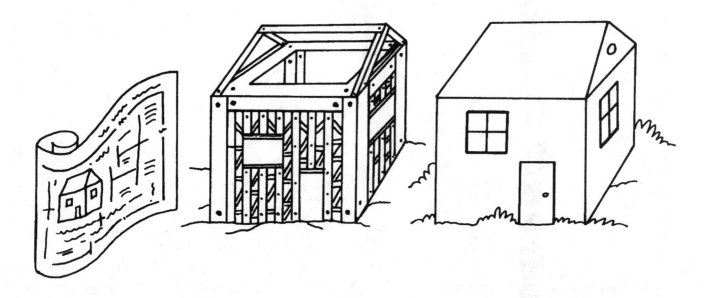

26

Operation Analysis (cont.)

It helps to make a list of possible factors when dividing an operation into stages. Naming the main junctures helps you decide what the main stages and substages should be. For example, imagine that you are taking a space flight through our known solar system. Leave Earth and make your first stop on our moon. Then fly past Venus to land on Mercury. From Mercury fly past Venus and Earth and land on Mars. Then return to Earth. The operation has three junctures of contact and three junctures of just coming close. First choose your ordering factor. Will it be points of actual contact or vicinity of Venus? Your analysis, which will look like an outline, will vary accordingly.

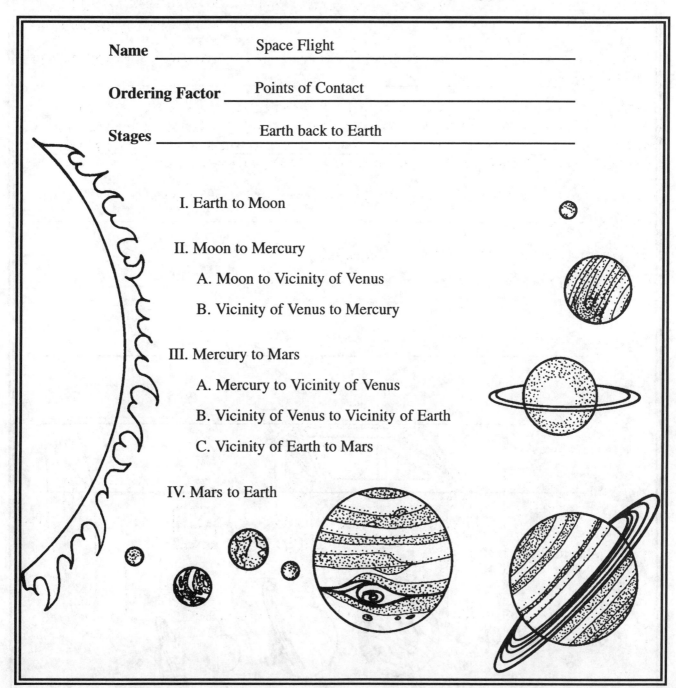

Name _____ Space Flight

Ordering Factor _____ Points of Contact

Stages _____ Earth back to Earth

    I. Earth to Moon

    II. Moon to Mercury

       A. Moon to Vicinity of Venus

       B. Vicinity of Venus to Mercury

    III. Mercury to Mars

       A. Mercury to Vicinity of Venus

       B. Vicinity of Venus to Vicinity of Earth

       C. Vicinity of Earth to Mars

    IV. Mars to Earth

Now try it (page 28) with an ordering factor of vicinity of Venus.

Abstraction

Name _____ Date _____

Operation Analysis *(cont.)*

I. Earth to Mercury

    A. _____

       1. _____

       2. _____

    B. _____

II. Mercury to Mars

    A. _____

    B. _____

    C.` _____

III. Mars to Earth

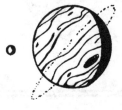

Name _____ Date _____

Operation Analysis *(cont.)*

Make an operation analysis for a planned birthday party. Fill in the the stages listed on the appropriate lines below.

Stages

1. Arrange Entertainment
2. Bake Cake
3. Send Invitations
4. Decide on Necessary Supplies
5. Gather Prizes
6. Set Date and Time
7. Prepare Invitations
8. Buy Groceries
9. Make Grocery List
10. Plan Games

Planning a Birthday Party

I. _____

   A. _____

   B. _____

II. _____

   A. _____

   B. _____

III. _____

   A. _____

   B. _____

   C. _____

Group Name_____ Date _____

Planning a Business

(This final exercise may serve as a culminating activity for the term.)

Individually, write a list of possible products you could profitably sell. In your group, decide on one product from the lists or create an imaginary product. Make a structural analysis of it to show how the parts relate to each other and form the whole.

Name the product, draw its picture, and make a structural analysis diagram. (Use pencil so that you can make changes easily.)

Possible Products	Estimated Cost of Production

Drawing of Your Product

Name _____ Date _____

Planning a Business *(cont.)*

Name the main qualities of your product. What sort of thing is it? On which rung of the abstraction ladder does it rest comfortably? Under sports equipment or cleansers? Above dog brushes?

Place your product in a classification diagram that shows it in relation to other similar products. Generate a list of similar products and horizontal sorting factors.

Your Product

Are there several possible specimens in your product's category? If so, is your product superior to them? It should be. Is the category itself profitable? Stable?

Name _____ Date _____

Planning a Business *(cont.)*

Form a corporation to produce, distribute, and sell your product. Make an operation analysis of the necessary stages.

Name of your corporation:_____

Write a vision statement such as "Our Williwigs will never fall apart" or "Williwigs are always delivered on time."

_____

_____

Make several sample operation analyses such as the following:

"Danigoes, Inc."

I. Marketing the Product

    A. Test market small group.

    B. Get customer feedback.

    C. Make appropriate changes.

II. Expanding the Market

    A. Plan advertising campaign.

        1. Calculate costs.

        2. Determine appropriate media.

    B. Plan distribution of product.

III. Managing Production

    A. Hire needed employees.

    B. Look at your business upside down and sideways.

    C. Predict problems.

    D. Solve problems by looking for the second and third right solutions.

Decide as a group which operation analysis is the best for your product. Then compare your diagrams with those of other groups and revise for improvement.

Name _____ Date _____

Writing About Abstraction

On the lines below, write a paragraph on how you can use the abstraction ladder to make your life easier. Brainstorm ideas in your group first; then write, beginning with a general statement or problem and descending the ladder with sentences that support the general statement.

_____

_____

_____

_____

_____

_____

_____

_____

_____

_____

_____

_____

To score one another's papers, use the following guide:

1. The writer opens with a clear statement about one possible use of an abstraction ladder.

2. The writer follows with gradually more concrete statements that support the opening.

3. The writer includes at least three supportive statements.

4. Grammar and spelling are clear, if not perfect, and do not interfere with the reader's comprehension.

All Four Points = A

Introduction

Physical science is primarily concerned with matter and energy. Earth science is primarily concerned with the Earth's relationship to other objects in space *(astronomy)*, to Earth's atmosphere *(meteorology)*, to its solid outer and liquid inner parts *(geology)*, and to its oceans *(oceanography)*. Life science is primarily concerned with living things—plants and animals. All sciences are interrelated. All sciences are attempts to satisfy human curiosity.

Read the paragraph below from "Will to Believe," by William James. Discuss what meaning you can extract—even if you do not understand all the words. It will become easier to understand if you take it apart sentence by sentence and make a few guesses. Then you will see how it relates to the study of science. Underline the words you would like to understand.

> *Man's chief difference from the brutes lies in the exuberant excess of his subjective propensities. His preeminence over them lies simply and solely in the number and in the fantastic and unnecessary character of his wants— physical, moral, aesthetic and intellectual. Had his whole life not been a quest for the superfluous, he would never have established himself so inexpungeably in the necessary. And from the consciousness of this, he should draw the lesson that his wants are to be trusted, that even when their gratification seems furthest off, the uneasiness they occasion is still the best guide of his life, and will lead him to issues entirely beyond his present powers of reckoning. Prune down his extravagances, sober him, and you undo him.*
>
> *—William James*

Now that you've discussed James' paragraph, read the following paraphrase on page 35 to see whether it agrees with your interpretation of the original.

Introduction *(cont.)*

Paraphrase of William James

Man's chief difference from other creatures lies in his eagerness— countless interests in all directions. His mastery over other creatures on earth lies simply and solely in the number of his wants which come from his imagination and are not necessary for survival. These desires are physical, moral, artistic, and intellectual. Had his whole life not been a search for things beyond what he needs for survival, he would never have established himself so surely. From knowing this, he should conclude that his wants are to be trusted, that even when they seem almost impossible to attain, the resultant uneasiness is the best guide of his life, and will lead him to issues entirely beyond his present powers of discovery and reasoning. Cut down his enthusiastic, extravagant, seemingly worthless searching, and you undo him.

Science is a search in all directions for regularity, pattern, and order. Science attempts to make sense of disorder, and to do that it must enthusiastically and extravagantly reach beyond what is already known.

Science needs analysis and synthesis, not necessarily in that order. You may come up with a light bulb-flashing synthesis first and then analyze the steps that led you to your insight. For example:

◆ You scampered up the abstraction ladder when you noticed that the birds in your back yard behaved in many ways like the dinosaurs. Is there an evolutionary connection? What are on the lower rungs of the ladder? _____

_____

◆ You notice that everyone in your class was born in the same year. Why does this uniformity exist? _____

_____

◆ What happens to the mites in your bed when you go away on vacation? Do they starve without you? _____

_____

◆ There is an imaginary rubber band around two people fighting. It stretches as they back away from each other and then snaps them back together to resume the battle. It stretches and snaps until it breaks and the fight is over. Why does the fight stop?

_____

◆ You notice . . . _____

_____

Name _____ Date _____

More Than One Right Answer

The next time you ask someone what the answer is to some question in your mind, change what you say from "What is the answer?" to "What are the answers?"

An idea, answer, or thought is like a single word or a musical note. Either one loses its effect when it stands alone.

What does the word "thinking" mean to you? Write whatever comes to mind. Try to expand from your first definition.

_____

_____

_____

_____

_____

_____

The technology of a given period affects the way people conceive of their world. It affects their art and their metaphors for mind and thought. The fast-growing technology of the 17th century was in the fields of optics and lens-making. People then described the mind as a mirror or a lens. The Freudian metaphor of mind borrowed from the universe of the steam engine locomotive. Images and thoughts billow up from the subconscious to the conscious in the same way steam moves from boiler to compression technology. The metaphor of thinking in the early 20th century came from telephone technology—the mind was described as a vast telephone-switching network with circuits and relays running through the brain.

Now we use the computer as a model, using such words as *input, output, information processing, retrieval, feedback, programming,* and *storage.* And we speak of the "information highway." A computerphile (lover of computers) said his wife had disappeared into the attic. "She was cruising the internet too long," he said. "I put her in storage but was unable to retrieve her." Can you blame her for not wanting to be "retrieved"?

What model of mental processing will be used in the 21st Century? _____

Try another:_____

And another: _____

And another: _____

Name _____ Date _____

Quests Begin with Questions

Scientists often start on a quest with a question: What if . . . ?

Asking "what if" questions is an easy way to get your imagination going. Here are a few:

◆ What if frogs became as large as people?

_____

_____

_____

◆ What if people lived to be only 20 years old?

_____

_____

_____

◆ What if dogs did not need sleep?

_____

_____

_____

◆ What if beanbag chairs were the only furniture schools had?

_____

_____

_____

◆ What if we had toes as long as our fingers?

_____

_____

_____

Make up some of your own "what if" questions and answer them on the back of this paper.

◆ What if . . . _____

◆ What if . . . _____

◆ What if . . . _____

The Scientific Process

The term "scientific process" simply refers to one of several systematic methods for proving or disproving a given question. Among other things, it means that we try to be careful, regular, and orderly when seeking an answer. If we are successful in doing this, others can follow our methods and come up with the same answers that we derive. Generally, these methods may be divided into a few orderly steps such as the ones that follow:

1. **Observe:** gather information, spread out your data so you can see it.

2. **Analyze:** take the subject apart with structural analysis, show relationships with abstraction ladder or classification diagram, show operation in time.

3. **Synthesize:** put pieces of analysis together in new ways.

4. **Test:** check your synthesis and revise accordingly.

There are two sorts of scientific observations: *qualitative* and *quantitative.* Qualitative asks what kind; quantitative asks what size or what number. In qualitative observation you abstract the quality of the thing and use descriptive words such as color.

In quantitative observation your descriptions are expressed in numbers that are useful in any kind of scientific endeavor—and universal. In the section on mathematics, you will see why numbers are abstractions.

Words are ambiguous, which means they may have two or more possible meanings. For example, the word *set* has more than 200 meanings. In problem-solving and other creative endeavors, ambiguity is essential as well as fun. In the section on language, you will see how it works and how words grow.

In quantitative observation we need to avoid ambiguity to make our observations clear. That is why standard measurements are used.

There are two systems of measurements used throughout the world, which is actually rather surprising when you realize that 80 languages are spoken daily in the city of Los Angeles alone. The English system of measurement uses inches, feet, and miles for length, ounces and pounds for weight, and quarts and gallons for volume. The metric system is a decimal system (units divisible by ten) and is the standard system of measurement in scientific observation. In the metric system a meter is a unit of length, a kilogram is a unit of mass, and a liter is a unit of volume. Greek prefixes are used in each case. *Kilo* as in kilometer means a thousand meters, *centi* as in centimeter stands for one one-hundredth of a meter, and *milli* as in millimeter stands for one-thousandth of a meter. Time is measured in seconds in both systems.

Mass is the measurement of the amount of material in an object. Mass is measured on a balance and is not affected by gravitational force. A unit of mass in the English system is the *slug,* about thirty-two pounds.

The Scientific Process *(cont.)*

Weight is affected by gravity or gravitational force.

You can lose weight by moving to a weaker gravitational force such as the moon.

The most commonly stated wish of teachers of science in high school is for students to come into their classes with open minds about science.

The following page is an exercise in forming a concept. Each group has a stack of cards of quotations relating to a problem. The cards contain statements which are positive and negative examples of attitudes that affect success in science classes. Each group will divide the stack in two categories and then write a statement of the concept the group has formed. Write each concept on the board and reach consensus for the class. Note how you climbed the abstraction ladder to write a concept.

Name _____ Date _____

The Two-Categories Game

Problem: Jane wants to go to college and major in history. She knows she has to pass high school chemistry but dreads taking it. Read the quotations on the cards and separate the stack into pairs as they relate to Jane.

Once your group has agreed on which of two piles each card should be placed, write two general statements that say what each of your stacks shows.

Cards

"Math is so much easier than science. Either the answer's right or it's wrong."	"The most important process in science is asking questions: how, why, how many, when."
"It takes some practice to understand and imagine the relative sizes of stars and electrons."	"The volume of my body would fit in the gas tank of my uncle's Cadillac."
"Ever since first grade when the teacher wouldn't let me count on my fingers, I've hated math. So, as it turns out, I'm just no good at science."	"There's so much I don't know about science and stuff; I'll never be able to learn it all."
"Scientists explore, letting what they discover lead them. They don't look for "right" answers."	"I could, if I had to, calculate the volume of the oceans on Earth."
"Volume is volume. I like to turn it up real high when I'm in a car."	"Women can develop the patience to make accurate measurements in science and learn how math, English, and science are alike."
"My second grade teacher said I was really good at drawing. I guess it comes naturally. My parents are both artists."	"I don't know why we have to learn the metric system. My father never talked to me about science."
"In science classes it's important to find the right answer before you continue on."	"I need to learn how to analyze dimensions. It will make school easier for me."
"I just can't imagine how big a star is. They look pretty small from down here."	"How many electrons can you fit on the head of a pin?"
"I can do math okay, but the stuff you have to do in science doesn't have anything to do with math."	"Since I don't even know what I don't know about science, I should probably learn that first."

Physical Science Overview

Physical Science is primarily concerned with *matter, energy,* and *motion.* All three are abstractions that cover a multitude of things and functions.

You have noticed by now that words change in meaning when they change context, as well as when they go up or down the rungs of the abstraction ladder.

In the language of physical science, *matter* is everything in the universe that takes up space.

Matter moves from one place to another or changes from one substance to another because of energy.

Matter is in constant motion whether or not you can see it. Matter can be analyzed structurally and classified. *Energy* can be measured and classified. *Motion* lends itself to operation analysis.

Matter has four states:

◆ Liquid   ◆ Solid   ◆ Gas   ◆ Plasma

Plasma occurs when the temperature of gas becomes so high that particles break apart into electrically charged pieces. The outer layers of stars are in a state of plasma.

Matter is the stuff of the universe. Energy is the capacity to move matter or charge matter. Energy never disappears. It simply changes form.

Energy is either potential or kinetic. Potential energy is the energy of position. When something appears not to be in motion, we say it has potential energy. When it appears in motion, we say the energy becomes kinetic.

Motion is change. Speed equals distance divided by time. Velocity is speed and direction.

Name _____ Date _____

Physical Science Observations

Take a minute to look around the room. Direct your viewing to include concrete illustrations (quite low on the abstraction ladder) of matter, energy, and motion, and write a paragraph describing what you have observed. Be sure to include the forms of the matter, the forms of the energy (potential or kinetic) and the motion—the effects of the energy on your chosen matter.

Observations

_____

_____

_____

_____

_____

_____

_____

_____

_____

_____

_____

_____

_____

_____

Critique one another's paragraphs on the basis of the following scoring guide; then rewrite the paragraph and submit it for your portfolio.

Scoring Guide

1. The writer describes at least three concrete examples of matter he has observed and the form of each.

2. The writer describes at least two forms of observed energy.

3. The writer describes the effects of the energy on the chosen matter.

4. The writer follows standard conventions of written language. In other words, each sentence is clear and relates to the others in the paragraph.

Name _____ Date _____

Scientific Terms Game

There is a vocabulary you need to know the rest of your life, if only to understand the news. Most words have several meanings (dependent on context); however, the meanings of the terms listed here are for scientific contexts. Some are more general (or more abstract) than others. To show their relationship—and for easy recall—fill in the diagram with its appropriate term or with the number representing it, whichever is easier.

Classify the following terms for easy recall. Fill in the horizontal sorting factors and pigeonholes with the numbers that represent each of the terms. Use a dictionary or the index of your science text and the diagram on the next page. When you have completed the diagram, study it and turn the page over to see how many terms you can write from memory. Analyze the ones you could not remember. Would changing their positions on the diagram help?

1. potential (matter in position)	7. astronomy	13. gases
2. oceanography	8. life	14. energy
3. animals	9. liquids	15. physical
4. Earth	10. plants	16. kinetic (matter in motion)
5. science	11. meteorology	17. geology
6. solids	12. cell	18. matter

Name _____ Date _____

Scientific Terms: Classification Diagram

Operation Analysis Model

(from *Creative Analysis,* page 103)

Use the following operation analysis as a model for one you will construct on the scientific process.

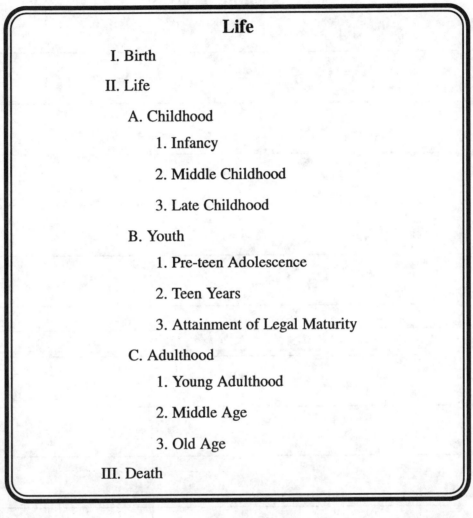

Life

I. Birth

II. Life

    A. Childhood

        1. Infancy

        2. Middle Childhood

        3. Late Childhood

    B. Youth

        1. Pre-teen Adolescence

        2. Teen Years

        3. Attainment of Legal Maturity

    C. Adulthood

        1. Young Adulthood

        2. Middle Age

        3. Old Age

III. Death

Now make a similar operation analysis by filling in the blanks on the next page with the following terms:

1. Scientific Process
2. relationship to others (classification)
3. hypothesize
4. describe theory
5. chart occurrences
6. quantitative
7. identify
8. analyze

9. qualitative
10. test
11. synthesize
12. describe
13. structural
14. meniscus
15. metric system
16. observe

(You will notice that the title has already been placed for you.)

Name _____ Date _____

Scientific Operation Analysis

Scientific Process

I. _____

   A. _____

      1. _____

      2. _____

   B. _____

      1. _____

      2. _____

      3. _____

II. _____

   A. _____

   B. _____

III. _____

   A. _____

   B. _____

IV. _____

Scientific Truth: A Continuous Search

The three main branches of science overlap, of course, as does science with all other subjects of study. The most important thought to keep in mind may be this: Nobody knows all the answers or perhaps even any "right" answers.

The famous Greek philosopher Aristotle (384–322 B.C.) said, "The search for truth is in one way hard and in another, easy. For it is evident that no one can master it fully nor miss it wholly. But each adds a little to our knowledge of nature, and from all the facts assembled there arises a certain grandeur."

Einstein's theories of 90 to 100 years ago have been put to the test and validated. What we know about Newton's law of gravity does not hold true for the black hole in space. In addition, two plus two is not always four.

The giants of scientific study have one thing in common, besides amazing brains. They knew what they did **not** know and approached the unknown with great affection for it. They were willing to stand on the shoulders of those who came before, and they had the courage to be unpopular.

Name _____ Date _____

The Nature of Matter

The following is a dense paragraph on the nature of matter. It may be hard reading. Stay with it and fill in the boldfaced terms on the appropriate lines of the abstraction ladder. The ladder will help you understand and remember the terms. You can see that the top rung of the ladder has the broadest or most general of the terms. The bottom rung has the narrowest or most specific.

From what scientists know so far, an **atom** *is the smallest particle of an individual element. An* **element** *is a substance that cannot be broken down into simpler basic substances. It has only one kind of atom. Each atom contains a tiny* **nucleus** *surrounded by rapidly moving* **electrons**. *Electrons are positioned around the nucleus within certain areas, or energy states, which are called* **shells**. *Each shell is a different distance from the nucleus. The nucleus is made up of tightly packed* **protons and neutrons**. *Evidence so far shows that protons and neutrons are made up of three* **quarks** *each. The total number of protons in a given nucleus determines the type of element. This number is called the* **atomic number** *of the element. The sum of protons and neutrons in a nucleus is called the* **atomic mass number**. *There are 106 naturally occurring atoms shown on the* **periodic table** *of elements. When they combine, they form* **matter,** *and matter is anything that has mass and takes up space. Mass is the amount of material in an object. It is measured on a balance which compares one amount of mass with another.*

Matter

Quarks

Name _____ Date _____

Structure Analysis of Helium

Now let us do a structural analysis of the element *helium*. Why? you ask. Because it is here, there, and everywhere…and easy.

Helium has two protons, giving it the atomic number 2, and two neutrons, giving it the atomic mass number of 4. Each proton and neutron has three quarks.

Effects of Observation

As you recall, there are two sorts of scientific observations—*qualitative* and *quantitative*. For both of these two, there are *micro* and *macro*. In macro observation you can describe and measure something without radically changing its properties. But how do you observe things so small that millions of them can fit on the head of a pin? It takes a mighty strong light, for example, to illuminate an atom of helium. Such a mighty beam of light is bound to have some effect on the helium electrons. It is comparable to someone entering a classroom with a fire hose to observe students. In the process of observation, the observer would hose the students out of the classroom even as he was trying to watch them.

Think about a time when something or someone you watched was affected by your watching. Being aware of your effect on things and people around you will enrich your life.

In your group discuss any such incidents that you may remember.

Choose one and write about it here.

_____

_____

_____

_____

_____

_____

_____

_____

_____

_____

_____

_____

_____

_____

Critique one another's paragraphs on readability; then correct your own and place it in your portfolio.

Name _____ Date _____

Interviews: Understanding Principles

The following exercise begins with reading and defining the principles. (That is what you have to do in every class.) Individually, choose two or three for homework interviews. Ask your instructor how to conduct interviews and to record and report results. Since you will be interviewing an adult about scientific principles, you may want to role-play an interview before actually conducting one.

First: Read all principles. Write your comments, questions, or paraphrases beside each principle. When you finish reading and writing about all of them, choose three for your interview. Do not select the same principles as the others in your group have chosen. Have a group leader attempt to distribute all the principles evenly among the members.

Second: Conduct your interview after school. Take extensive notes.

Third: Read the examples that follow (page 53) on how an English teacher might respond to each principle.

Fourth: Report the results of your interview to the class.

Fifth: Decide as a group and then as a class how you think your effort in this project should be evaluated.

Principles for Interviews	Comments, Questions, Paraphrase
1. Events in nature are the result of multiple cause-and-effect relationships. The laws and theories of nature—as they apply to motion, energy, change, conservation, and atomic structure—are simplifying generalizations in which a cause and an effect are related. These laws and theories are based on experience and verified either by experiment or by controlled, objective observations.	_____
2. Knowledge of cause and effect makes possible the prediction of events.	_____
3. Cause-and-effect relationships are universally applicable. A major goal of the scientist is to discover universal laws of nature as well as ordered patterns of diversity that have causal relationships.	_____

Interviews: Understanding Principles (cont.)

Principles for Interviews   **Comments, Questions, Paraphrase**

4. Predictions based on cause-and-effect relationships may also be made if the events are random. Some events in nature, however, occur in such random fashion that predictions concerning individual events can be made only with great uncertainty. One can predict many occurrences with a high degree of certainty by applying statistical techniques to the study of such random events. For example, one can predict the fraction of total atoms that will disintegrate in a given mass of radioactive atoms in a given period of time, but one cannot predict when a specific single atom will disintegrate.

5. Frames of reference for size, position, time, and motion in space are relative, not absolute. With increasing accuracy of instruments and techniques, measurements come closer to (but can never reach) absolute values. The most difficult quantitative concepts are those well beyond the level of intellectual comprehension: the numbers of atoms and stars or atomic and cosmic dimensions.

6. A kilogram is a unit of mass and is valuable because of its constant dependability regardless of its position in the universe. But it is also used as a standard unit of weight at the earth's surface where its particular value depends on the earth's gravitational field. When the kilogram is transferred to an environment away from the earth's surface, this standard unit of weight loses its earthbound value.

7. Matter is composed of particles that are in constant motion.

8. Energy exists in a variety of convertible forms.

9. Scientists use classification systems to bring order and unity to apparently dissimilar and diverse things. Matter is organized into units which can be classified into organizational levels.

10. Units of matter interact. Interaction and reorganization of units of matter always are associated with changes in energy.

       52

Interviews: Sample Responses

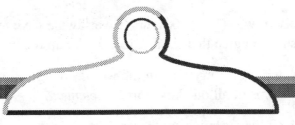

Suppose that the person you interview is an English teacher. Following are some of the things he or she might say about your chosen principle.

1. When I notice that my students are noisy and out of sorts as well as out of order, I look for the probable cause so that my response will have the effect I want. If the cause is frustration with the learning material, I can change the way I ask them to learn it. If it's the weather—hot dry winds, for example—I can change activities to counteract it, such as watching a cool (in more than one sense of that word) video.

2. From experience with cause and effect, I can predict that student behavior changes with changes in weather.

3. Students all over the world laugh and cry. Students come in all colors and sizes. When students go to high school they learn to walk. Before that, they run. The cause: incredible energy.

4. If students are threatened with punishment such as being kept after school, they are statistically apt to change their behavior to avoid the punishment. However, any given student at any time may choose to continue the behavior that will result in punishment.

5. The number of students in my classroom is reaching cosmic dimensions.

6. When one of my students is transferred to high school, he or she learns how to walk from class to class instead of running.

7. Young people are in constant motion. So are my thoughts as I try to keep track of my students.

8. The energy of my students converts from low in the middle of class to high at the end of the period.

9. Schools are organized into units and organizational levels. Students are grouped by age. Subjects are grouped by time. Teachers are scheduled by time and subject. Principals do the organizing of the school.

10. Imagine the world covered by a waterbed. Jump on it in one part of the world and it will expand outward in another.

Life Science: The Dynamics of Growth

How do plants and animals grow? To date, scientists worldwide have tested their hypotheses often enough with the same results to agree that six elements make up the building blocks of all living things.

You know already that the term for everything in the world, living and nonliving, is *matter;* that matter is made up of *atoms;* that atoms of all one kind form an *element.*

The six elements found in all living things are these:

✳ **carbon**	✳ **oxygen**	✳ **phosphorus**
✳ **hydrogen**	✳ **nitrogen**	✳ **sulfur**

These elements appear in a variety of compounds. In fact, there are more than five million known carbon compounds. Imagine the diagrams you would need to chart all those. (Other elements besides these six are necessary for life, but in extremely small amounts only.)

All living things on earth grow. All contain *compounds*—elements in combination. Water is one of those *compounds*—two parts hydrogen, one part oxygen. Carbon dioxide is another.

Carbohydrates are compounds made of carbon, hydrogen, and oxygen. *Fats* are compounds of carbon, hydrogen, and oxygen. *Proteins* are carbon compounds with nitrogen. They arc the raw materials your body uses to repair itself. They form the scab over the cut. Those proteins that control chemical activities are called *enzymes.* All are necessary for growth.

Plants and animals are made up of cells. Cells can be reproduced only by other living cells. Each cell has a *nucleus* surrounded by *cytoplasm,* a thick fluid. Floating in this fluid are *ribosomes* (which make protein) and *mitochondria* (which provide energy). What look like tiny bubbles are called *vacuoles.* Vacuoles store food, water, and waste. The *cell membrane* is the gate controlling what goes in and out of the cell.

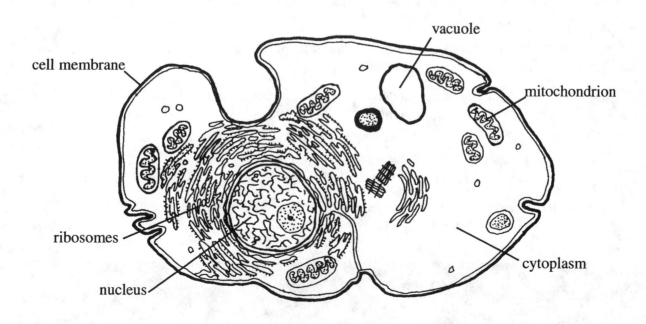

Name _____ Date _____

Life Science: The Dynamics of Growth *(cont.)*

With the appropriate words below, fill in the lines of this structural diagram of a cell.

      A. **cell membrane**   B. **nucleus**   C. **ribosomes**

      D. **cytoplasm**   E. **mitochondria**   F. **vacuoles**

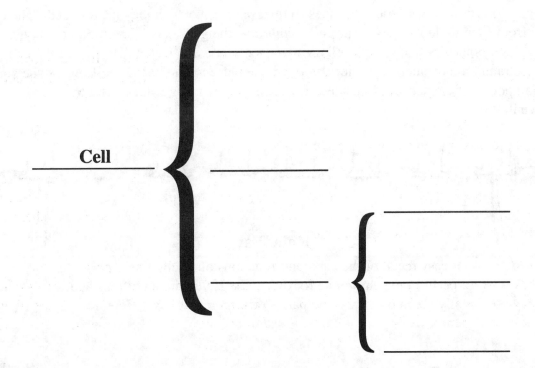

Plant cells differ from animal cells in that they have walls around their cell membranes. Some plant cells contain *chloroplasts*. Within the chloroplasts is *chlorophyll* which gives plants their green color. Chloroplasts store solar energy and mitochondria release energy.

What do cells do all day while you are moving, resting, and growing?

The nucleus is in control. It is the center for cell reproduction that makes you grow. It contains DNA—which is easier to say than *deoxyribonucleic acid*. Look at the parts of this formal term for DNA. What separate words or word parts are represented in it?

1. _____

2. _____

3. _____

4. _____

Life Science: The Dynamics of Growth *(cont.)*

DNA is the code that controls what the cell does while you are carrying out your life activities. One thing the cell does is make *proteins*. Proteins are made in the *ribosomes* in the *cytoplasm*. A chemical message carried in code from the DNA in the *nucleus* directs the ribosomes, telling them which proteins to make. As you recall, the proteins aid growth, repair cell parts, reproduce, and make enzymes.

The *mitochondria* break down food molecules to release energy which they have stored. The cell uses the energy from food to do its work. The *cell membrane,* the gatekeeper, lets food and oxygen in and wastes out. The molecules that enter a cell are always dissolved in water. They enter the cell by diffusion, the random movement of molecules from one place to another. *A molecule* is the smallest part of a compound of elements. Molecules move from an area of greater concentration to an area of lesser concentration.

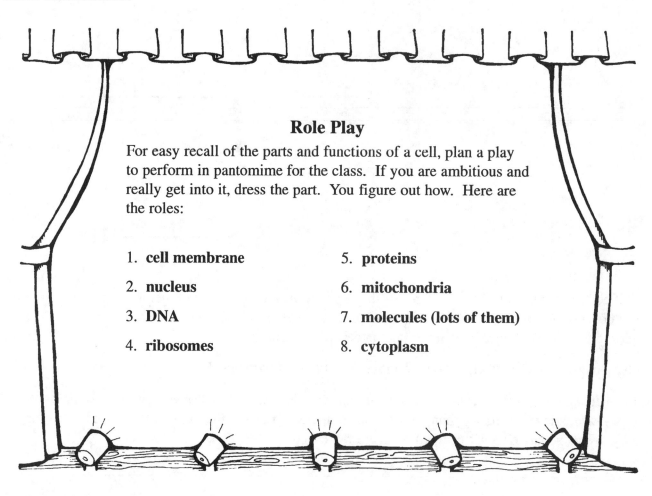

Role Play

For easy recall of the parts and functions of a cell, plan a play to perform in pantomime for the class. If you are ambitious and really get into it, dress the part. You figure out how. Here are the roles:

1. **cell membrane**
2. **nucleus**
3. **DNA**
4. **ribosomes**

5. **proteins**
6. **mitochondria**
7. **molecules (lots of them)**
8. **cytoplasm**

• Combine with another group and choose roles.

• Study the function of your chosen role.

• Perform for the class and let the class guess which part each person plays.

Name _____ Date _____

Earth Science

In the next several pages, you will have to read actively, marking words you do not understand, writing questions, putting ideas in your own words, drawing pictures and diagrams.

Structure

Plants and animals grow; dunes and rocks form. The Earth has been forming and reforming for eons. From bits and pieces of information taken from all branches of science, we now have a model of the structure of the Earth underneath the part we can see.

The outside layer of Earth is called the crust. It is relatively thin and consists of *sedimentary* rocks, (mud, clay, and sand) *metamorphic* rocks (changed by heat and pressure deep inside the Earth), and *igneous* (from Latin for *fire)* rocks or volcanic rocks. We can't see the crust because it is mostly covered with small rocks, soil, and sand. Seas and oceans also cover the crust. Its average thickness is 32 kilometers (20 mi.), although it varies considerably from place to place. The boundary between the crust and the layer below is called the *Mohorovicic Boundary* after the scientist who discovered that *seismic waves* suddenly increase because of a change in the density of the rocks.

Vibrations from earthquakes are called *seismic waves*. There are three kinds of seismic waves: *primary* or P waves that cause material to vibrate back and forth, *secondary* or S waves that cause material to move from side to side and do not pass through liquid, and *surface* or L waves, which move slowly along the Earth's surface, much like ocean waves.

Thoughts, Questions, Sketches

Earth Science *(cont.)*

Structure

The layer below the crust is called the *mantle.* It is relatively thick and goes from the bottom of the crust down to about 2,900 kilometers (1,798 mi.). It is made of solid rock, far more dense than rocks in the crust. The mantle itself consists of layers. It has rigid upper and lower layers surrounding a middle layer that moves slowly, like thick syrup. The mantle makes up 84 percent of the Earth's volume and about two-thirds of the Earth's mass. During the Ice Age, huge amounts of ice accumulated in some places. The weight of this ice caused the crust and upper mantle to sink. Now that the ice has melted, the crust and upper mantle are moving back upward. With increasing or decreasing weight, the crust and upper mantle sink or rise as if they were floating on liquid. But since P seismic waves go through the central mantle, it cannot be liquid. It is more like a plastic material that is solid but can flow over a long time.

The center part of the Earth is a large, dense *core.* It begins below the mantle and continues the remaining 3,400 kilometers (2,108 mi.) to the center of the Earth. The core has a solid inner part surrounded by a liquid outer layer. Both are thought to be made of iron and nickel. The core makes up 15 percent of the Earth's volume and about one-third of its mass.

Thoughts, Questions, Sketches

Name _____ Date _____

Earth Structure Diagram

On the appropriate lines of the structural diagram below, write the following terms.

1. **Earth**   2. **liquid core**   3. **mantle**

4. **crust**   5. **core**   6. **sedimentary rock**

7. **rigid rock layers**   8. **metamorphic rock**   9. **thick, moving liquid**

10. **solid core**   11. **volcanic rock**

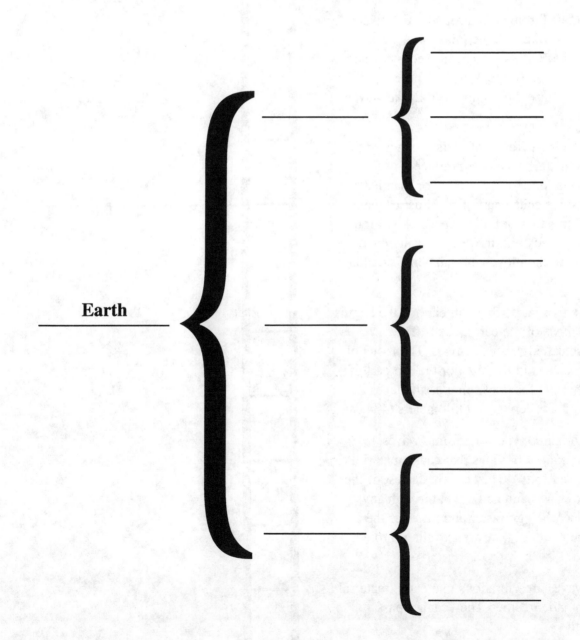

Name _____ Date _____

Earthquakes

Read the following information on earthquakes, making notes and sketches along the side. Then, in your group draw a diagram of the Earth (see page 62) showing the forces of subduction at work. (The prefix "sub" in Latin means under, and "duction" from the Latin "ducere" means to lead.)

Label your drawing and include all the terms that are in italics. Compare your drawing with the others in your group and create a composite drawing to show to the rest of the class. You may want to vote as a class to choose the best one.

Explanation

Vibrations move through the ground much like ripples move in water. Sometimes there are larger vibrations in the Earth's surface caused by a sudden release of energy within the Earth. These vibrations can cause the ground to roll like waves on the ocean.

An earthquake is the result of a disturbance in the Earth. Large disturbances are produced by a movement deep in the Earth's crust or mantle. Various pressures cause part of the crust or mantle to be pushed together or pulled apart. A section breaks along a crack and moves, releasing energy. The place where the movement happens is called a *fault.*

The place along a fault where an earthquake begins is called the *focus* of the earthquake. The vibrations are called *seismic waves.* The focus of most earthquakes is in the crust or the top part of the *mantle,* but the focus of some earthquakes has been measured as deep as 700 kilometers (434 mi.).

Remember the three types of seismic waves. *Primary waves* are vibrations that cause material to vibrate back and forth. They are the fastest of the three seismic waves and can travel through any material. Also, they go faster and faster as the density of the material they are traveling through increases.

Secondary waves are vibrations that cause material to move from side to side. They cannot pass through liquid.

Notes & Sketches

Name _____ Date _____

Earthquakes *(cont.)*

Explanation

Surface waves are the slowest of the waves. They move along the Earth's surface much like waves on the ocean. These waves cause the most damage from an earthquake.

Seismic waves move outward from the focus. Moving downward, some seismic waves travel all the way through the Earth. Moving upward, some waves reach the surface. The place on the surface directly above the focus is called the *epicenter.*

Since 1992, *subduction zones*—where 50-mile (80 km) thick slabs of one great *tectonic plate* dive under another—have greatly affected how Earth scientists think about the forces that shape the surface of the Earth.

Imagine a 50-mile (80 km) thick plate that has been cooling off in a gigantic refrigerator. Then push this plate through some warm rocks. The cold plate will slowly sink because it is of higher density than the rock.

Picture it. This plate carries water to the sediments and to the rock underneath. As the plate goes deeper into the Earth's mantle, the waters are forced up, melting the hot rocks that are between the two tectonic plates.

Not only water, but chemicals and gases, too, are pushed from the Earth's crust down into the mantle, then back up again.

The hot rocks between the plates melt and rise to the surface as lava or *magma.* Earthquakes that come from deep inside the Earth, like the one in Bolivia in June 1994, are caused by these tectonic plates that have subducted—sunk deep into the mantle.

Earth scientists now believe that gases such as carbon dioxide and methane are carried down by the cool, dense, subducting slabs into the mantle and come back up much later, even millions of years later, erupting in volcanoes or into ocean trenches.

Notes & Sketches

Name _____ Date _____

Earthquake Diagram

Now, when you stand in a meadow in springtime watching the tall grasses waving in a gentle wind and butterflies dancing in the sunlight, think about the drama of these gigantic plates subducting under your very feet. You could well wonder where in the world those waters and gases will poke through the Earth's crust next.

In the space below, place your diagram showing those forces of subduction, according to directions on page 60.

62

Name _____ Date _____

Electromagnetic Fields

Below is a related selection about a curious kind of lightning that comes from within the Earth and has very strange effects on people. It is from *The Power of Place* by Winifred Gallagher.

Ball Lightning

The Earth has a magnetic field that causes compasses to point north. The magnetic field is believed to originate from the liquid outer core. When your car radio suddenly pours out static as you drive by high tension wires, you know you are moving through an electromagnetic field.

We animals have magnetic fields, also. Our bodies are electric. Whales, dolphins, and birds travel on magnetic roads. Neuro-scientists have correlated effects of the Earth's magnetic fields on human behavior and health.

We have all seen lightning course the sky. Some of us have seen lightning that looks like glowing blue, white, red, or orange globes up to a foot in diameter floating through the air, even through walls, before vanishing. This is called ball lightning and usually occurs with a thunderstorm.

Pyott Kapitsa, a Soviet Nobel winning physicist, suggested that ball lightning was made of plasma—electrically charged atoms of gas, the stuff around stars—lit up by naturally occurring fields of electrical energy. Scientists have since confirmed his theories by using microwave-like devices. They now accept the reality of what they had once considered to be voodoo science.

The geomagnetic field coming from the Earth's magnetic core, which sets the compass and protects us from radiation from space, is complicated and changeable. The changes come from the variation in conductivity of materials in certain places. The energy in these places where there are natural deposits of conductive materials is usually only twice as strong as the normal electromagnetic field, but, spread out over a large area, there is a cumulative effect. These places are called "magnetic deviation zones," and navigators know them because their compass needles are pulled away from true North.

Notes, Comments, Questions

_____

_____

_____

_____

_____

_____

_____

_____

_____

_____

_____

_____

_____

_____

_____

_____

_____

_____

Name _____ Date _____

Electromagnetic Fields *(cont.)*

Ball Lightning *(cont.)*

All creatures feel the influence, especially birds. Birds, like whales and dolphins, have magnetic organs they use for direction when they migrate. Geomagnetic irregularities skew their sense of direction. Along with light, the Earth's geomagnetic field, perhaps, keeps plants and animals synchronized with the solar system.

In humans, the pineal gland, which regulates behavioral cycles by producing tides of chemicals in response to light signals, can also detect changes in electromagnetic fields. Research in this relationship has just begun. What we have so far leads us to consider that distorted perceptions and psychic experiences may occur when an electromagnetic signal is received directly by the magnetic part of the brain.

For example, one time a group of medical professionals were on a hunting trip in a remote valley in New Mexico. Suddenly they saw all the cactus plants turn red. Frightened, they fled the area, and all the plants turned back to green. Returning cautiously, they saw the cacti were once again red. They had stumbled on a small area with a lot of magnetic materials in the ground. The changed magnetic field altered the hunters' pineal glands, and possibly that of an electromagnetic organ, which caused neurological changes in their sight.

In the late 1960's hundreds of thousands of people reported seeing the Virgin Mary and/or other celestial beings in Zeitoun, Egypt, not far from Cairo. Photographs at the site actually showed glowing blobs of light. Michael Persinger, a professor of neuroscience in Canada, examined seismological records and discovered that a year before people began seeing the celestial beings there was an unprecedented increase, by a factor of ten, in seismic activity near Cairo.

Notes, Comments, Questions

_____

_____

_____

_____

_____

_____

_____

_____

_____

_____

_____

_____

_____

_____

_____

_____

_____

_____

_____

_____

64

Name _____ Date _____

Electromagnetic Fields *(cont.)*

Ball Lightning *(cont.)*

After studying the conditions of 6,000 strange events such as fish or frogs raining from the sky, haunted houses, and UFOs, Persinger found that many could be explained by natural hypothesis. He is inclined to think that the Earth's processes affect the nervous system in humans as well.

We are conditioned to think that fish stay in water, that rocks do not pop out of the Earth, that cacti do not turn red. When we are confronted with such strange occurrences, we try to make sense of them. Both religion and science provide structured ways to do that. Until the development of plasma physics, we had no scientific way to think about ball lightning.

As a scientist would, Persinger decided to look not at isolated incidents but at the patterns they fit into. He plotted the place and time of numerous sightings of strange occurrences as well as the geophysical activity at those same places and times—and he discovered a strong correlation.

Persinger writes, "Profound perceptual changes, such as hallucinations, can result from the induction of substantial direct current into the body. That's why many people who've had such experiences report that they woke up after being unconscious—they'd been knocked out. If the current, perhaps generated by tectonic strain deep within the Earth, is too intense, the person dies of a heart attack or seizure, and is reported as having had an attack or seizure of the normal kind."

After reviewing more than 1,200 reports of balls of light that move about, Persinger believes that most UFO encounters can be explained—and predicted—by solar and seismic variables. "Between August 2 and 7 in 1972, for example, massive sunspot activities shocked the Earth hard enough to knock it off its orbit," he said. "On August 10, multicolored fireballs, probably consisting of plasma, were reported. On August 19, a major UFO flap began, with many people reporting luminous objects, football-shaped spacecraft, and the like."

Notes, Comments, Questions

_____
_____
_____
_____
_____
_____
_____
_____
_____
_____
_____
_____
_____
_____
_____
_____
_____
_____
_____
_____
_____
_____
_____

Electromagnetic Fields *(cont.)*

Ball Lightning *(cont.)*

Mountain tops in the Andes of Chile periodically blaze with glowing and flashing lights accompanied by popping, sizzling sounds. The "Andes Lights" were first reported in *Scientific American* in 1912 and more recently were seen by Gemini astronauts. Unusual energy fields are generated by the conductive sediment in mountains and in large basins such as those found in Utah, New Mexico, and the Black Hills of the Dakotas where many strange sightings have occurred.

Beneath the Earth's surface massive geophysical forces seethe with activity, changing the electromagnetic forces in any given area. Most of the unusual experiences people have reported over the years resemble those described by people whose brains have been stimulated during surgery or in attacks of nonconvulsive epilepsy. In both cases, people reported strong smells, loud noises, depersonalization, and visions. The combination of real external physical events and unreal ones from a stimulated brain produces a confusion of the rational and the bizarre.

This leads us to consider that our everyday perceptions are affected by our brains interacting with the environment. The one influences the other. And this process began in the complex world of the womb.

Is it any wonder that people can't see eye to eye?

Notes, Comments, Questions

_____

_____

_____

_____

_____

_____

_____

_____

_____

_____

_____

_____

_____

_____

_____

_____

_____

_____

_____

Writing Prompts

(Read both prompts before you choose.)

Prompt A

Think of a time when you saw something very strange that had a profound effect on you. Describe the incident. Include many concrete details. Did anyone else have the same or similar experience? What did you think at the time about the incident? Include your thoughts on the effect of geomagnetic fields on human perception. Draw a conclusion. In other words, go up and down the abstraction ladder in your writing. Make sure you have many concrete details and one or two generalizations. (After some thought, if you cannot recall such an incident that you or someone close to you has had, go to the second writing prompt.)

Write a draft first. Have it critiqued in your group according to the following scoring rubric; then rewrite to make it clearer and better.

(A score of 5 on the following guide would be an A; 4, a B; 3 , a C; and 2, a D.)

Scoring Rubric for Prompt A

1. The writer opens with a detailed description of the incident(s).

2. The writer includes reactions of other people.

3. The writer includes specific details that support the generalities or build to a general conclusion.

4. The writer includes some thoughts on the effects of geomagnetic fields on human perception.

5. The writer uses clear sentences, varies his sentence patterns, and makes few errors in standard conventions of written language.

Prompt B

Write a summary of the above passage on ball lightning. Include the main ideas in your own words. Include what you think the overall meaning suggests to you about future research.

Scoring Rubric for Prompt B

1. The writer opens with a general and lively introduction of the topic.

2. The writer includes all the main ideas of the selection in his own words.

3. The writer speculates on future research, using specific details.

4. The writer uses clear sentences, varies his sentence patterns, and makes few errors in standard conventions of written language.

In this case, a 4 would be an A; 3, a B; 2, a C; and 1, a D.

(When scoring a partner's paper, you may write "one-half of number 2," for instance, if you feel the writer has not quite lived up to the obligations of that point but has not ignored it either.)

Language and Growth

The well-known editor and writer William Zinsser thinks of writing as a way to learn. He says, "Probably no subject is too hard if people take the trouble to think and write and read clearly. Maybe, in fact, it's time to redefine the Three R's—they should be reading, writing, and reasoning. It's by writing about a subject we're trying to learn that we reason our way to what it means. Prior knowledge of a subject isn't a requirement for writing; only the ability to arrange information in narrative order."

How do we arrange information in narrative order? We do it by looking for relationships, both known and unknown.

In this section, we will dance back and forth between meaning and reasoning, reading and writing for fun, and reading and writing to learn. We were not born knowing how to write. We were born knowing how to learn how to write. And we begin with the word.

The Dynamic Growth of Meaning

Listen to a toddler talk. He or she speaks in sentences with a familiar rhythm and pitch, but his words are unintelligible. He hears and repeats the music of the language of his home long before he gets the sense of it. How happy he is when he can communicate both music and lyrics.

As we grow and develop in using language, we learn how well it functions as . . .

1. a way to lie when truth-telling seems dangerous to our health,

2. a pump handle that releases and controls our feelings,

3. a source of beauty (myths, stories, poetry, religious ceremony) and humor,

4. as a tool for thought. Without clear language there can be no clear thought, no abstraction ladder, no analysis nor synthesis, no cold soft drinks, and no hot pizza.

With language—and with knowledge of how languages work throughout the world—we have the most powerful tool in the universe at our disposal. Few people know the range of its power. Most people take language for granted. For instance, have you ever speculated about why language must be ambiguous?

Ambiguous comes from the Latin meaning "going about, to wander about." Anything said to be ambiguous is susceptible to multiple interpretations. Ambiguity is not necessarily bad. In fact, the words with the most meanings turn out to be the workhorses of any language.

Think of all the uses of a hammer. Now, how many uses can you find for the word *set*? In the Oxford English Dictionary, there are more than two hundred meanings listed for *set*. Such a useful word!

Name _____ Date _____

Language and Growth *(cont.)*

Write 10 sentences below, each with a different sense of the word *set*. Help each other come up with new uses.

1. _____

_____

2. _____

_____

3. _____

_____

4. _____

_____

5. _____

_____

6. _____

_____

7. _____

_____

8. _____

_____

9. _____

_____

10. _____

_____

If we had to have 200 different words for *set* (and for others of our most useful terms), we would need to have a vocabulary that exceeds our brain's capacity. As it is, we have a core group of words we use every day that change in meaning according to context. Moreover, if words did not have multiple meanings, quite a few comedians would be out of work.

Stephen Wright, one comedian, says, "I parked my car in a tow-away zone. Came out after the movies and discovered they had towed away the zone." Also, he asks, "What's another word for *thesaurus*? Have you heard the old joke about the magician who walked down the street and turned into a drugstore? The humor in such sentences, of course, depends on the listeners' understanding of the multiple meanings of individual words and phrases. Often called a "play on words" or a "pun," this deliberate use of a word with double meaning is one of the delights of language use.

Semantics: How Words Grow

Words grow: they change meaning in new contexts. This is called *semantic growth*. Semantics is the study of meaning. Each time you ask, "What do you mean by that?" you are acting like a semanticist. By being aware of how our minds work in all languages and how words change meanings in different contexts, we become alert to the many possibilities of miscommunication. The most successful people in the world know they must not assume they have communicated what they intended to communicate simply because they chose their words carefully. They know it is wise to question the receiver and to expect ambiguity.

◆ For example, when a politician proclaims he is working for "law and order," at what level of abstraction is he speaking? Does he mean what a Supreme Court justice would mean by the same phrase?

◆ A prisoner wants law and order in the prison system; a policeman wants it on the streets. An historian looks at patterns of relative law and order.

◆ A philosopher may advocate breaking one law to obey a higher law, thus creating disorder for the sake of a higher order.

◆ At the bottom of the ladder, from where our politicians usually speak, "law and order" means catching criminals and putting them in prison.

◆ Near the top of the ladder, law means that body of rules a tribe or nation agrees to. Sometimes nations break their own laws for the sake of international order. One obvious example of this is "diplomatic immunity." This is the practice of one country granting the visiting officials of a friendly nation limited freedom from punishment for breaking any laws during their visits. (A citizen may be arrested and fined for breaking a traffic law, but a visiting ambassador may not.) This is widespread practice around the world for most countries which exchange ambassadors or maintain diplomatic relations with one another. It is practiced as a type of "courtesy" to promote peace and harmony among nations.

◆ Therefore, the answer to "What do you mean by that?" depends on the level of abstraction.

(The following is from *Creative Analysis*, pages 129–131.)

Semantic growth is the process by which old words take on a new sense and often become ambiguous. There are seven sorts of semantic growth, and they are fun to play with.

The first kind of semantic growth is *sensory, affective* and *logical* similitude. *Similitude,* as the name implies, is when meaning is transferred to a new thing or quality because it refers to a similar thing or quality.

Sensory similitudes involve experiences of vision, hearing, taste, touch, and smell. We notice that the sound of a motorcycle engine resembles the roar of a lion, so we say the engine "roared." The old sense of "roar" is that of the lion, since we knew about lions before we invented engines. We notice that the flap between shoelaces resembles a dog's tongue so we speak of the "tongue" of a shoe.

Name _____ Date _____

Semantics: How Words Grow *(cont.)*

In your group, see if you can come up with three words that have added new meanings or senses because of *visual similitudes*. (Hint: waves)

1. _____

2. _____

3. _____

An *affective similitude* is a name which has been transferred to a thing or quality because it refers to an emotionally similar thing or quality. Affective similitudes involve such qualities as love, fear, anger, beauty, disgust, awe. A pretty girl used to be called a "flower" and an offensive person a "skunk." Name three words that have changed in meaning through affective similitude. (Hint: honey)

1. _____

2. _____

3. _____

A *logical similitude* is a name which has been transformed from one thing or quality to another because both have a similar relationship to a third thing or quality. In logical semantic growth, A is to B and C is to B. For example, the old sense of "ring" is a round piece of jewelry for a finger. That "ring" we find on the inside of the bathtub that we are supposed to clean off is another sense of ring. It does not look like the original, so there is no visual similitude, but it goes around the tub as a ring goes around a finger.

Logical similitudes are harder to dredge up, but see what you can come up with, anyway.

1. _____

2. _____

3. _____

Name _____ Date _____

Semantics: How Words Grow (cont.)

The second kind of semantic growth is *irony*. Ironies reflect the differences between things or qualities instead of the similarities. An irony is a name of the thing that has been transferred to an opposite thing. The expression "not" sometimes follows an ironic statement such as, "I wish school lasted until five p.m. every day—not." Or someone might say, "The sun comes up every day." If you respond to that statement with "Really? How amazing!" you would be using the word *amazing* in an ironic or opposite sense.

What ironies can you think of?

1. _____

2. _____

3. _____

The third kind of semantic growth is *abstraction-concretion*. Remember the abstraction ladder? An abstraction is a name which has been transferred from a thing to one of its qualities. A concretion is a name which has been transferred from a quality of a thing to the thing itself. Consider "orange." It is an abstraction taken from the fruit to represent a color. A "uniform" is a concretion from the abstract quality of uniformity.

In the following sentences determine which type of semantic growth occurs, an abstraction or a concretion:

Old sense: He broke the law when he ran across the street.

New sense: Politicians who call for law and order usually win at the polls.

(Since the second sentence suggests the whole inclusive idea of many specific laws, we say it is an abstraction. It is not concrete or specific.)

The fourth, fifth, and sixth kinds of semantic growth are *genus-species, structurals,* and *operationals*. Remember the three sorts of analysis? The classification diagram shows genus-species relationships. In semantic growth, a word that stands for the class is transferred to the specimen, such as fish. Or, the word that stands for the specimen is transferred to the genus in a new context. "I like my car," and "The fourth car of the train is derailed."

Structurals show the relationship of a part to its whole. It is a name which has been transferred from a part to a whole or from a whole to a part. We use the word "almond" to refer to a nut when originally it was the name of the tree that produced the nut. This is a case of a whole-to-part structural sort of semantic growth because the name of a whole has been transferred to one of its parts.

Operationals show the relationship of a whole operation such as "hunting" that includes the beginning movement, middle chase, and retrieval of the thing hunted to one stage of the operation, as in "Hunting for the rabbit, the man jumped the fence."

Name _____ Date _____

Semantics: How Words Grow *(cont.)*

On the lines following each pair of sentences, identify the type of semantic growth based on the six types described so far: (from *Creative Analysis,* pages 138–145)

◆ Similitudes (Indicate which kind—sensory, affective, or logical.)

◆ Ironies

◆ Abstractions-concretions (Indicate which.)

◆ Genus-species (Indicate which.)

◆ Structurals (whole-to-part or part-to-whole)

◆ Operationals

Old sense: Of all the cats in the jungle, the lion is king.

New sense: My cats make a mess of their kitty litter.

1. Semantic growth type: _____

Old sense: Will you go to the dance with me?

New sense: They left after the first dance.

2. Semantic growth type: _____

Old sense: Cotton grows well in warm climates.

New sense: It's hard to separate the cotton from the seeds.

3. Semantic growth type: _____

Old sense: Class ended at 3:30.

New sense: The class started in September and ended in June.

4. Semantic growth type: _____

Old sense: A cane is a walking stick made from cane.

New sense: He had a plastic cane.

5. Semantic growth type: _____

Name _____ Date _____

Semantics: How Words Grow *(cont.)*

Old sense: The bees were buzzing around the lilies.

New sense: The alarm clock was buzzing.

6. Semantic growth type: _____

Old sense: Some Indians are brave.

New sense: The settlers were attacked by braves.

7. Semantic growth type: _____

Old sense: My neighbor's cow had a calf last week.

New sense: The young of elephants, walruses, and cows are calves.

8. Semantic growth type: _____

Old sense: The wolf bared his teeth in a ferocious smile.

New sense: Look at the cut on that toy poodle. Doesn't he look ferocious?

9. Semantic growth type: _____

Old sense: Take the rubbish to the dump.

New sense: Semantic growth is all rubbish.

10. Semantic growth type: _____

Old sense: Cows swat flies with their tails.

New sense: Look at the tail on that comet!

11. Semantic growth type: _____

Old sense: He toasted marshmallows in the fire.

New sense: She toasted her freezing feet by the fire.

12. Semantic growth type: _____

74

Name _____ Date _____

Semantics: How Words Grow *(cont.)*

> **Old sense:** A lemon is a citrus fruit.
>
> **New sense:** Her dress was lemon and white.
>
> 13. Semantic growth type _____

> **Old sense:** He was painting the seat of the chair.
>
> **New sense:** Come on in. Pull up a seat.
>
> 14. Semantic growth type _____

So far, you have discovered six of the seven ways that words grow. Before we begin to explore the power of metaphor, let's play with senses.

◆ How many senses do you have?

◆ You may answer "five" if you assume that one is talking about physical ways we perceive our environment.

◆ Or you may answer "six" if you include ESP.

◆ Suppose one asks, "How many senses does the word *set* have?" The answer is "It has more than two hundred."

◆ The context (the words surrounding "sense") gives us the sense of it.

◆ What do you do when you make sense of something? Or what do you mean when you say, "That just doesn't make sense!"?

Language is wonderfully fluid. Let's go back to "How many senses do you have?"

The usual answer is five: *taste, touch, smell, hearing, seeing.* Some say the sixth sense is *kinetic*— some sort of muscle-knowing. Others say it is an intuitive sense—a *metasense* (meta meaning beyond, thus creating an umbrella word to cover all other possibilities).

Some call it *synesthesia,* the spilling over from one sense to another common in all languages. Examples of synesthesia occur when we speak of *loud colors* and *sharp sounds, velvety voice* and *cold light, sweet music* and *bitter words.*

Name _____ Date _____

Semantics: How Words Grow *(cont.)*

Without using any of the given examples, discuss and then write four examples of synesthesia, using the visual sense to describe music, the auditory sense to describe food, the taste sense to describe a personality, and touch sense to describe interior decor.

Synesthesia Examples

1. (*seeing*—music)

   _____

   _____

2. (*hearing*—food)

   _____

   _____

3. (*tasting*—personality)

   _____

   _____

4. (*touching*—interior decor)

   _____

   _____

Following is the word game Ping Pong which illustrates synesthesia from Ann Bertoff's *Forming, Thinking, Writing.*

Beside each word below, quickly write "ping" if it seems fitting, or "pong." There is no right or wrong. Let your own whimsy be your guide.

_____	1. athletic shoes	_____	9. Toyota Camry
_____	2. blue jeans	_____	10. sneakers
_____	3. apple	_____	11. soccer
_____	4. cat	_____	12. Buick
_____	5. hot soup	_____	13. day
_____	6. night	_____	14. lemon
_____	7. tennis	_____	15. dog
_____	8. ice cream		

Compare your choices with others in your group. How many differences and agreements do you see? Explain your choices to each other.

The purpose of the game is to reveal how slippery language is. (Is "slippery" ping or pong?)

76

Name _____ Date _____

Semantics: How Words Grow *(cont.)*

The previous activity leads us to metaphor as a way for words to grow. We will begin with proportional analogies from *Creative Analysis* (page 149).

When we write one is to two, or one over two, or one to two, or 1/2 or 1:2, we are thinking of a ratio or relation between one and two of the kind that makes up fractions in arithmetic. If we say that one is to two as three is to six and write 1/2 = 3/6, or 1:2::3:6, we call the comparison a *proportion* or *proportional analogy*. But, as you may have discovered in formal testing, we do not have to stick to numbers. We may say that a dog is to a pup as a bear is to a cub or a cat to a kitten.

A shell is to a hermit crab as a hut is to a hermit. It is the relationship that is similar between the two pairs, not the pairs themselves. For example, fill in the fourth word in each of the following pairs from those available beside the blank.

1. $\dfrac{\text{covers}}{\text{book}} = \dfrac{\underline{\hspace{2cm}}}{\text{person}}$ head, clothes, man, nose

2. $\dfrac{\text{lion}}{\text{animal}} = \dfrac{\text{flower}}{\underline{\hspace{2cm}}}$ plant, grass, roots, rose

3. $\dfrac{\text{violence}}{\text{activity}} = \dfrac{\text{melancholy}}{\underline{\hspace{2cm}}}$ evening, cruelty, mood, silence

4. $\dfrac{\underline{\hspace{2cm}}}{\text{honesty}} = \dfrac{\text{emotion}}{\text{love}}$ falsehood, passion, witness, virtue

5. $\dfrac{\text{wave}}{\text{crest}} = \dfrac{\underline{\hspace{2cm}}}{\text{peak}}$ water, top, moving, mountain

6. $\dfrac{\text{arrival}}{\text{departure}} = \dfrac{\underline{\hspace{2cm}}}{\text{death}}$ life, person, birth, train

7. $\dfrac{\text{feather}}{\text{bird}} = \dfrac{\text{scale}}{\underline{\hspace{2cm}}}$ fish, fin, animal, man

8. $\dfrac{\text{man}}{\underline{\hspace{2cm}}} = \dfrac{\text{bird}}{\text{beak}}$ head, mouth, body, leg

9. $\dfrac{\text{seven}}{\text{number}} = \dfrac{\text{large}}{\underline{\hspace{2cm}}}$ size, small, whale, distance

10. $\dfrac{\underline{\hspace{2cm}}}{\text{harvest}} = \dfrac{\text{landlord}}{\text{rent}}$ farm, barn, cow, farmer

Semantics: How Words Grow (cont.)

11. $\dfrac{\text{moon}}{\text{planet}}$ = _____planet_____   sun, space, galaxy, comet

12. $\dfrac{\text{spectator}}{\text{audience}}$ = _____letter_____   number, alphabet, sentence, pencil

13. $\dfrac{\text{flower}}{\text{weed}}$ = _____   plant, swan, bird, buzzard
                               crow

On the lines below, write the thoughts that went through your mind as you tried to figure out which word to choose in the previous exercise. For example, in the problem, *army: soldier as faculty: school, education, student,* or *teacher,* you may choose "teacher" by saying, "An army is where soldiers belong, so a faculty is where teachers belong." Or, "An army is made up of soldiers and a faculty is made up of teachers."

Write the sentence(s) that went through your mind for six of the 13 analogies.

1. _____

   _____

2. _____

   _____

3. _____

   _____

4. _____

   _____

5. _____

   _____

6. _____

   _____

Turn the page over if you need more room.

Compare answers and thoughts with others in your group and your teacher's key.

Name _____ Date _____

Semantics: How Words Grow *(cont.)*

Simile and Metaphor

Although you will rarely see proportional analogies in the above form except on tests, they are a major part of language and function as the most complex way that words take on new meanings.

Metaphor describes the relationships implied in analogies. They reflect relationships. A is to B as C is to D.

When you say calculus is a branch of mathematics, the word "branch" is used metaphorically. A branch is to a tree as calculus is to mathematics.

Similes differ from metaphors only in the manner of their statement. A is like B or C or D. When we use similes, there is no immediate semantic growth; the words do not take on new meanings. We expressly state a comparison: She reminds me of a silver dollar.

In the Australian phrase, "Joe really spat the dummy that time," meaning Joe was so angry he exploded, the comparison is direct. He is like a baby who is so frustrated he/she spits out the pacifier.

Nearly all of our most common words have senses which are metaphorical. Consider how often we use the word *heart*. The heart of a person or a frog may differ in structure, but not in function. The functions are analogous; the use of the word for both frog and man shows the analogy. We also have *the heart of a city, the heart of celery*—you take it from here:

1. The heart of _____

2. The heart of _____

3. The heart of _____

4. The heart of _____

5. The heart of _____

We speak of. . .

◆ a high profile, meaning. . .   _____

◆ a high voice, meaning. . .   _____

◆ a high price, meaning. . .   _____

◆ high treason, meaning. . .   _____

◆ and high ambition. meaning. . .   _____

Each use of *high* signifies a relationship which is analogous with the relationship of every other use of the word.

Name _____ Date _____

Semantics: How Words Grow *(cont.)*

Name and provide examples of three metaphorical uses for the word *cut*. (*He cut to the left* might be one example.)

1. _____

2. _____

3. _____

◆ ◆ ◆ ◆

Name and provide examples of three metaphorical uses for the word *wing*.

1. _____

2. _____

3. _____

◆ ◆ ◆ ◆

Name and provide examples of three metaphorical uses for the word *dead*.

1. _____

2. _____

3. _____

◆ ◆ ◆ ◆

Name and provide examples of three metaphorical uses for the word *right*.

1. _____

2. _____

3. _____

◆ ◆ ◆ ◆

Compare your choices with others in your group. Turn this page over and write from memory what the difference is between simile and metaphor. Make sure you include "analogy" or "analogous" in your definition.

Name _____ Date _____

Semantics: How Words Grow *(cont.)*

To discover how metaphor can be used as a means to solve a problem, let us look first at where metaphors live, then at where they can take you.

Metaphors inhabit what we call three "universes of discourse," or to put it another way, "worlds covered by the range of things, thoughts, and words."

The *analogical universe* is the universe from which we borrow familiar relationships and terms. Take the word *coat*. In the analogical universe it is something we wear in cold weather. When we use it as a "coat of paint" we have transferred the word to a new context which we call the *contextural universe*.

The *meta-universe* is a comprehensive universe which includes the other two. It is a genus which contains the others as species. A metaphor is the result when the terms of one universe are transferred to another. (In Greek, *metaphor* means transfer.)

Metaphors (found in all of Shakespeare's plays) are not just pleasing additions to speech or writing. They are instruments of creative thinking. When you take a familiar relationship, such as boots to kicking, and put it in a new context when building a computer, you realize you just can't turn a computer on and have it work—you have to "boot up" the system.

Metaphorical analysis enables us to see and understand the unfamiliar as well as gain additional insight into the familiar by controlling language symbols, and, therefore, the thoughts they stand for.

> **Why would I say that without language you can't have pizza?**

Discuss that question in your group, write your final answer below, and compare it with that of other groups.

_____

_____

_____

_____

_____

_____

_____

_____

Name _____ Date _____

Semantics: How Words Grow *(cont.)*

(Creating functional analogies from *Creative Analysis*, page 173)

Choose one of the following exercises, one that no one else in your group chooses, or work with a partner on two of them.

1. Write a metaphor using *flower growing* as your analogical universe and *child rearing* as your contextural universe.

◆ ◆ ◆ ◆

2. Design a *grocery* store display analogous to an *Egyptian pyramid.*

◆ ◆ ◆ ◆

3. Write a metaphor using *warfare* as your analogical universe and *courtship* as your contextural universe.

◆ ◆ ◆ ◆

4. Apply the principle of *musical harmony* to a *social situation.*

◆ ◆ ◆ ◆

5. Write a metaphor using *fishing* as your analogical universe and *salesmanship* as your contextural universe.

◆ ◆ ◆ ◆

6. Write a metaphor using *anatomy* as your analogical universe and *law enforcement* as your contextural universe.

◆ ◆ ◆ ◆

7. Write a metaphor using *space travel* as your analogical universe and *finding a career* as your contextural universe.

◆ ◆ ◆ ◆

8. Think of several areas in which the principle of the *thermostat* might be applied.

◆ ◆ ◆ ◆

9. What suggestions might you make to improve a system of *automobile traffic regulation*, reasoning by analogy from the human *circulatory system?*

◆ ◆ ◆ ◆

10. Write a metaphor using *weather* as your analogical universe and *dreams* as your contextural universe.

◆ ◆ ◆ ◆

11. Paint or draw *a picture* which is analogous to *a piece of music* you enjoy. Or compose a piece of music which is analogous to a work of art you admire.

◆ ◆ ◆ ◆

12. Invent a new *water sport.* (What will it be analogous to?)

◆ ◆ ◆ ◆

13. Write a simile using *gold mining* as your analogical universe and *scientific research* as your contextural universe.

◆ ◆ ◆ ◆

14. Write a metaphor using *our galaxy* as your analogical universe and *something closer to your life now* as the contextural universe.

82

Name _____ Date _____

Semantics: How Words Grow *(cont.)*

Famous Quotations About Words

1. From Rabelais: *Then he threw on deck handfuls of frozen words, and they looked like pearly pills in different colours. We saw there words of gules, words of sinople, words of azure, gilded words. When they were warmed a little in our hands, they melted like snow, and we actually heard them.*

   What kind of a transfer is this—metaphor or simile?

   _____

2. From Jean Giono: *Before writing down a word I taste it as a cook tastes the ingredient which he is going to put in his sauce; I examine it against the light as a decorator examines a Chinese vase which he wants to set against a suitable background; I weigh it as a chemist who pours into a test tube a substance capable of blowing up everything; and I use only those words whose intimate flavour and whose power of evocation and resonance are known to me.*

   And this—metaphor or simile?

   _____

3. From Charles Osgood: *The word is the father of the act. If we are going to avoid blood then we must learn soon to curb our tongues, to end this orgy of self-indulgence in words with warheads.*

   Metaphor or simile?

   _____

4. From William Shakespeare: *Thou has frightened the word out of his right sense, so forcible is thy wit.*

   Paraphrase:

   _____

   _____

   _____

   _____

5. From Balzac: *What a fine book one could write by relating the life and adventures of a word! It has no doubt received various impressions from the events in which it has been used; it has evoked different ideas in different places.*

   What is the analogical universe here?

   _____

Name _____ Date _____

Semantics: How Words Grow (cont.)

Famous Quotations About Words *(cont.)*

6. From Victor Hugo: *Present everywhere, a dwarf hidden beneath our tongues, the word holds the globe under its heels and enslaves it.*

   What do you think this means?

   _____

7. Victor Hugo again: *Words are the mysterious passers-by of the mind.*

   How does this remind you of "a slip of the tongue"?

   _____

8. From Carl Sandburg: *Look out how you use proud words. When you let proud words go, it is not easy to call them back. They wear long boots, hard boots. Look out how you use proud words.*

   What do you think he means by "proud words"?

   _____

9. From Shelley: *Words are like a cloud of winged snakes.*

   Metaphor or simile?

   _____

10. From E.M. Forster: *The world created by words exists neither in space nor time though it has semblances of both, it is eternal and indestructible, and yet its action is no stronger than a flower.*

    What does this mean?

    _____

11. From Thomas Hobbes: *Words are wise men's counters—they do but reckon with them, but they are the money of fools.*

    Paraphrase:

    _____

    _____

    _____

    _____

12. From Ivor Brown (just to enjoy): *The craftsman is proud and careful of his tools; the surgeon does not operate with an old razor-blade; the sportsman fusses happily and long over the choice of rod, gun, club, or racquet. But the man who is working in words, unless he is a professional writer (and not always then), is singularly neglectful of his instruments.*

Semantics: How Sentences Grow

We have been looking at semantic growth and the main purposes of language. When it comes to writing, we have to consider the structure of sentences. It may seem as if you have been studying parts of speech since day one, and perhaps you are right (allowing for just a bit of exaggeration, of course). Nevertheless, let us review a few important elements.

There is a vocabulary for sentence structure that makes your life easier once you learn it. You have to know the names of the tools you use in the kitchen or the garage, so you might as well learn the names of the language tools you use everywhere.

First, there are two sorts of sentences, *compound* and *complex*. Can you remember which is which?

(**Answer**: A *compound sentence* consists of two or more independent clauses. Independent clauses contain both subject and matching verb form. A *complex sentence* consists of an independent and subordinate clause. A subordinate clause may contain a verb form, but not one that matches the noun's form. A subordinate clause cannot stand alone as a sentence.)

A *sentence* consists of a *noun* and a *matching verb*, at least, and usually has many other words such as you see in this sentence.

Let us begin with sorts of *nouns*. There are at least nine sorts of nouns you should know.

A *common noun* is just as it seems, common. You can make a plural of it. It is usually quite concrete. You can see, feel, hear, smell, or taste it.

A *proper noun* is the formal name of somebody or some place or some thing. It is always capitalized.

An *abstract noun* is just as it seems, abstract. It stands for a quality or time span that you cannot see, feel, hear, smell or taste.

An *appositive* is a noun that explains another nearby noun.

A *pronoun* stands for a noun.

A *possessive pronoun* stands for a noun but implies possession.

A *compound noun* is two nouns linked together, with or without a hyphen.

A *collective noun* represents a group of something—for example, a gaggle of geese.

A *noun clause* is a group of words which includes other parts of speech but functions as a noun in the sentence.

Name _____ Date _____

Semantics: How Sentences Grow (cont.)

Identify the kinds of nouns the words below represent:

Term	Type of Noun
1. chocolate-almond	_____
2. crowd	_____
3. chair	_____
4. Massachusetts	_____
5. their	_____
6. year	_____
7. flock	_____
8. fun	_____
9. baseball	_____
10. whoever ate my yogurt	_____
11. field	_____
12. Paris	_____
13. flower	_____
14. he	_____
15. why we did that	_____
16. Brasilia, the capital of Brazil,	_____
17. its	_____
18. An ichthyornis, a fish-eating bird,	_____

When you finish, compare your responses within your group, turn the page over, and write new examples for as many forms of nouns as you can remember.

86

Name _____ Date _____

Semantics: How Sentences Grow *(cont.)*

| This sentence no verb. |

What is wrong with the sentence in the box above?

For your classification diagram (see page 88) of verb forms, here are the sorts followed by the specimens.

Sorts

◆ *Action verbs* show physical or mental action as well as ownership.

◆ *Linking verbs* connect, or link, the subject of the sentence with the words that describe or identify it. Common linking verbs: *to be, taste, become, seem, sound,* or any verb linking an adjective to the subject.

◆ *Helping verbs* help make the meaning of the main verb more specific. "Be, do, have, may, will, would, can" are examples.

◆ *Transitive verbs* are followed by a direct object, as in "The runner ran the track," with *track* being the direct object.

◆ *Intransitive verbs* are not followed by a direct object, as in "The runner ran around the lake." Here the verb is followed by a prepositional phrase.

◆ *All verbs* have four parts:

  Present—"I see you."

  Present participle—"I am seeing you every day now."

  Past—"I saw you."

  Past participle—"I have seen you."

  ("To see" is an *irregular* verb, in that the spelling changes from the past to the past participle. In *regular* verbs, those two parts are spelled the same.)

Specimens

Since some verbs function as both transitive and intransitive, this distinction is not included in the classification diagram on the next page. Use these words for that diagram.

1. eat	6. have run	11. feeling
2. seemed	7. have been	12. is
3. dropped	8. skipping	13. castigated
4. lose	9. saw	14. dousing
5. ate	10. winning	15. have seen

Name _____ Date _____

Semantics: How Sentences Grow (cont.)

Fill in the blanks of this classification diagram with the appropriate specimens listed on the previous page.

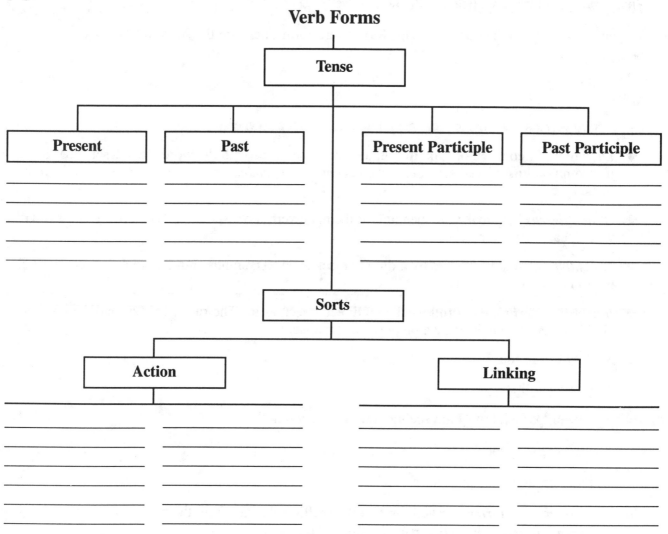

Compare your placement of terms in your group.

More on Verbs

Participle phrases, both present and past forms, can function as adjectives.

"The picture *hanging on the wall* looks fuzzy. Dust *gathered over the years* has blurred it."

Gerunds are verb forms that end in "ing" and function as nouns. They are not to be confused with participles that function as adjectives.

Example: *Swinging over construction sites is dangerous. Swinging* is the gerund functioning as the subject of the sentence. *Over construction sites* is a prepositional phrase telling where. *Is* is the linking verb of the sentence and *dangerous* is the adjective linked to the gerund, *swinging.*

Name _____ Date _____

Semantics: How Sentences Grow *(cont.)*

All verbs have tenses—the time expressed by the verb. As you have seen, we have *present, past,* and *future.* They are easy. But we also have progressive forms of verbs that show action over time such as these: "We *are studying* language today" for present progressive and "We *were studying* science yesterday" for past progressive.

Perfect tenses are used to show that one event happens before another time or event. For example, in "The books have arrived" the verb is present perfect and in "The books had arrived" the verb is past perfect.

Infinitives are formed from "to" and the basic form of the verb. Infinitives can be used as nouns, adjectives, or adverbs. You can distinguish infinitives from common prepositional phrases that begin with "to" by noticing whether the "to" is followed by "the." *(a.) He runs to exercise. (b.) He runs to the store.* Which is which?

If followed by "the," it is a _____.

Beside each of the following sentences, write the form of the italicized word(s). Choose from the forms listed below the sentences.

1. *Swimming* is cool.   1. _____

2. The book *lying* on its side is torn.   2. _____

3. The book *dropped.*   3. _____

4. He *dropped* the book.   4. _____

5. The man *has come* home.   5. _____

6. The man *had come* home.   6. _____

7. What are you *looking* for?   7. _____

8. *To be*, or not to be, that is the question. 8. _____

9. You *are* sick.   9. _____

10. She *worries* a lot.   10. _____

11. He *could* be lost.   11. _____

12. The electric lines *were buzzing* all night. 12. _____

- past progressive
- past perfect
- linking
- present participle
- infinitive
- intransitive
- participle as adjective
- action
- helping
- present perfect
- transitive
- present progressive

Now that you know the vocabulary, you need not feel insulted when someone accuses you of dangling your participles.

The Function of Fiction

Storytelling is as old as mankind, as old as language itself. In the beginning we had the tale, the lyric poem, the epic poem, the myths, and the plays that fed our souls, our yearning to explore mysteries.

The novel, meaning "new," grew out of those traditions and gained in popularity in the 19th century.

Remember the four functions of language?

1. as a way to lie when truth-telling seems dangerous to our health

2. as a pump handle that releases and controls our feelings

3. as a source of beauty (myths, stories, poetry, religious ceremony) and humor

4. as a tool for thought (Without clear language there can be no clear thought, no abstraction ladder, no analysis nor synthesis, no cold soft drinks, and no hot pizza.)

Consider number three above. Beauty is a source of pleasure. You read for pleasure, you dance for pleasure, and you watch television for pleasure.

Now, pleasure is an abstract term that has all kinds of concretions. When you say "I like XYZ," it is similar to saying "XYZ gives me pleasure."

- What do you like about watching movies?

- What do you like about reading stories?

- What do you do when you read a story or watch a play or movie?

You willingly suspend your disbelief for the duration of the novel, play, or film.

Storytelling is an unsung necessity of life. Try to imagine a day without it. Imagine sports without anyone talking about the game afterwards—or beforehand. Imagine taking a big risk, succeeding, and then telling no one about it. Remember the fish that got away? Just how big *was* it?

- The stories we tell define us.
- The stories we tell ourselves are a kind of fiction in that we select those among many that "fit" our evolving definitions of ourselves.
- The stories we hear place us in relation to others.

Name _____ Date _____

The Function of Fiction *(cont.)*

Read the following pages on fiction. Underline all words you do not understand and write them in the column to the right along with related questions or thoughts.

Features of Fiction

During sleep, we dream our stories and restore our brains after a day of bombardment.

$$\frac{\text{Dreams}}{\text{Life}} = \frac{\text{Fiction}}{\text{Reality}}$$

Stated as a metaphor: Dreams are the indirect lights that illuminate our perceptions just as fiction illuminates and gives meaning to reality.

Has anyone ever told you to stop daydreaming? My mother used to chide me about it regularly. Neither she nor I knew my imaginative life while awake was as important to my mental health as my dreams during sleep.

◆ ◆ ◆ ◆

The information we glean from fiction is of the deepest sort. Information from fiction adds meaning and relevance to the facts of life.

Question: What is the difference between fiction and nonfiction?

Answer: Fiction, though made up from the imagination, reveals more truths about human nature than true stories which merely reveal the surface.

◆ ◆ ◆ ◆

Think of a work of fiction that still resonates for you, still has meaning. In other words, what is your favorite story?

What did it tell you about yourself? (That is a hard one to answer. Think about it for a few days.)

Notes

_____

_____

_____

_____

_____

_____

_____

_____

_____

_____

_____

_____

_____

_____

_____

_____

_____

_____

_____

_____

_____

_____

Name _____ Date _____

The Function of Fiction (cont.)

Features of Fiction

When I was eleven years old, I read a novel called *A Tree Grows in Brooklyn*. I loved it, and it still resonates for me. It told me about life in ways that real people would not. Years later, as I came to know myself better, I realized I had intense curiosity about other people's inner lives, their deepest thoughts, their secrets. When I read fiction, I enter the minds of the characters and share an intimacy with them I have rarely experienced with real people.

What villain in real life would ever tell you the source of his villainy? Or even see himself as a villain? Hitler thought he was a heroic savior of the German race.

What hero knows his villainous side?

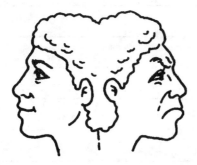

If the fiction is true, its truth resonates—that is, it continues to echo in our hearts and memories. Not all fiction is true. Therefore, the responsibility of fiction writers is great. If the writer veers from the truth of his own perceptions to conform to ideology or to some commercial concept of vulgar mass taste, he ignores the truth of fiction and destroys the purpose of it.

Reading works that are safe and predictable does not ease endemic loneliness and does not help us define ourselves. Such works may occupy our time, but they do not resonate.

Nevertheless, when reading or watching either kind of fiction we willingly suspend our disbelief. A reader, listener, or watcher of stories makes a silent agreement with the teller of stories. The agreement: I will suspend my normal disbelief in order to enjoy your story.

Notes

_____

_____

_____

_____

_____

_____

_____

_____

_____

_____

_____

_____

_____

_____

_____

_____

_____

_____

_____

_____

_____

_____

_____

Name _____ Date _____

The Function of Fiction *(cont.)*

Features of Fiction

When Ray Bradbury in *The Martian Chronicles* writes about people from the Midwest of America moving to Mars, we willingly suspend our disbelief and feel the truth of his stories.

When the Disney Corporation produces yet another cartoon film, we believe those characters are real for the duration of the film.

That is the beauty of imagination.

- It cleanses the brain.

- It is temporary.

- It is under our control, normally.

- It is our will that suspends our disbelief.

In the space below, draw a picture of a fictional character you love:

Notes

_____
_____
_____
_____
_____
_____
_____
_____
_____
_____

What does this tell you about the nature of love?

Name _____ Date _____

Mythology

◆ Every family has its "myths," its stories that come down through the generations.

◆ Every country has its myths.

◆ Those organizations such as schools and corporations that build their own myths and publish them seem to function better than those that do not.

◆ What are the myths of your school?

Try collectively putting together a group of your own school myths. Begin by talking about what you have heard about your school over the years. What have you heard about other schools? How is your school unique?

Beginning with the abstraction of what you have heard about your school, write a few concrete examples to give body (and soul) to your myth. These concrete examples should be true in that they actually happened. The fiction comes in selecting the ones that best fit the myth that best describes your school, that gives the truth to your school.

We speak of "spin doctors," professional writers who put a spin on the news so it reflects what they want it to. When a defense lawyer wants to present his client in an innocent light, he digs out those facts that show the client's good character and ignores other facts. In other words, he selects what he wants to present. In that sense, we are all spin doctors. So go ahead and spin.

_____
_____
_____
_____
_____
_____
_____
_____
_____
_____

Combine what you have written with the writings of others in your group and then with that of all your classmates. Give a variety of drafts to your principal for the parent newsletter. Publish your final draft in the school newspaper.

Name _____ Date _____

What Is Plot?

Below is a famous definition from E.M. Forster's *Aspects of the Novel*. Underline major terms.

Let us define a plot. We have defined a story as a narrative of events arranged in their time-sequence. A plot is also a narrative of events, the emphasis falling on causality. "The king died and then the queen died" is a story. "The king died, and then the queen died of grief" is a plot. The time-sequence is preserved, but the sense of causality overshadows it. Or again: "The queen died, no one knew why, until it was discovered that it was through grief at the death of the king." This is a plot with a mystery in it, a form capable of high development. It suspends the time-sequence, it moves as far away from the story as its limitations will allow. Consider the death of the queen. If it is in a story, we say "and then?" If it is in a plot we ask "why?" That is the fundamental difference between these two aspects of the novel. A plot cannot be told to a gaping audience of cave men or to a tyrannical sultan or to their modern descendent, the movie public. They can only be kept awake by "and then—and then—"; they can only supply curiosity. But a plot demands intelligence and memory also.

In the space below, paraphrase the distinction Forster makes between *plot* and *story*. Use his example of the king and queen. Remember to comment on the importance of the question set up in the reader's mind.

_____
_____
_____
_____
_____
_____
_____
_____
_____
_____
_____
_____
_____
_____
_____

Name _____ Date _____

What Is Plot? *(cont.)*

In pencil, so you can easily change your mind, fill in the blanks on the diagram with appropriate numbers representing the generalizations and specifications and their relation to each other.

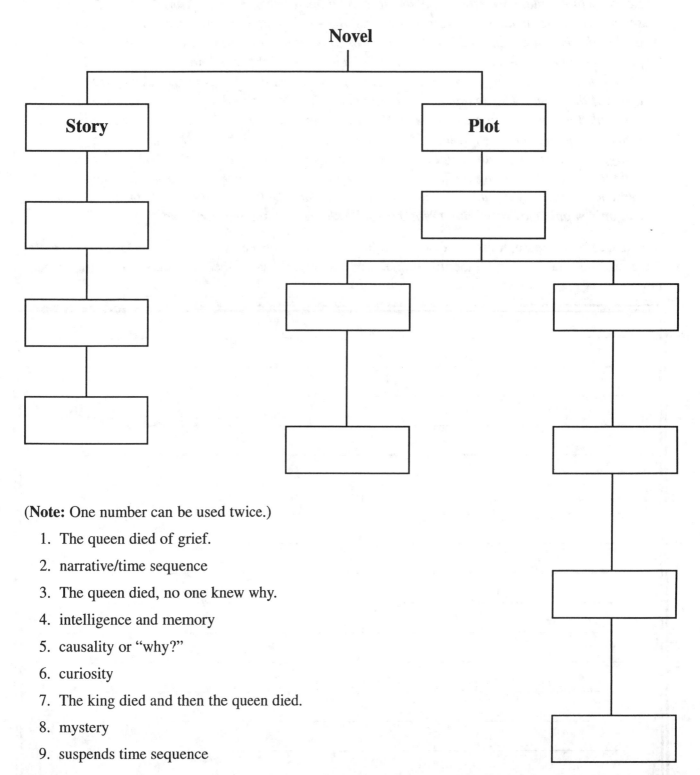

(**Note:** One number can be used twice.)

1. The queen died of grief.

2. narrative/time sequence

3. The queen died, no one knew why.

4. intelligence and memory

5. causality or "why?"

6. curiosity

7. The king died and then the queen died.

8. mystery

9. suspends time sequence

96

Name _____ Date _____

Writing About Friendship

Write a paragraph on friendship like Forster's definition of plot by filling in the blanks below with your own words. Then copy the whole paragraph. (Leave out or add any words that you want.)

Let us define friends. We can define acquaintances as those people we see regularly and whose company we usually enjoy. Neighbors and colleagues fall into that category. Friendship often grows out of acquaintanceship, but must include _____.

Friends can hurt your feelings in ways acquaintances cannot. My friends know I like to be on time and to fulfill all commitments. When one does not keep a promise to me, I'm hurt. I would not expect as much from acquaintances. Strong friendship survives _____ and even _____, as in marriage. Strong friendship requires time to develop and acceptance of the most _____ qualities as well as the most _____ qualities of the other. My best friend laughs at the same situations I laugh at, responds to my needs if she can, comes to me in her need, _____ too much, _____ , _____ and _____ .

Name _____ Date _____

Willing Suspension of Disbelief

◆ Have you ever won a dare? Regretted making a dare?

◆ Have you ever wanted something badly but would not let your parents know what it was?

◆ Have you ever dreamed of traveling through space?

◆ Think about space travel for a minute. What do you know about outer space?

Now, please suspend your disbelief as you read the following short story. Read slowly. Write your questions and comments in the space provided. Stop to doodle now and then. Draw a picture of the main character. Write whether you want more or less description of her.

Laddru's Dare
by Evelyn C. McNeilly

When Laddru of New Vaning, on the planet Drucan, turned fourteen, her father stood her against the wall of their hut and measured her. "You're sixty-six centimeters tall!" he exclaimed. "You've reached your full height, Laddru."

"That means I'm all grown up, doesn't it?" She hoped it meant she wouldn't be so lonely at school anymore.

Her father stroked her soft white hair. "Not necessarily," he replied. "There's more to it than that. There's learning how to make smart decisions. To grow means to know what you value . . ."

She wished she hadn't asked. This was his usual lecture. She picked up a brush to groom the long white, fur-like hair that covered her body. Her father's hair was tan in color, and her mother's light pink, but she'd been slowly taking pills to whiten hers and now it was pure, shimmering white.

Thoughts, Questions

_____
_____
_____
_____
_____
_____
_____
_____
_____
_____
_____
_____
_____
_____
_____
_____
_____
_____

Name _____ Date _____

Willing Suspension of Disbelief *(cont.)*

Laddru's Dare (cont.)

Thoughts, Questions

Also, although her mother knew nothing about it, Laddru had been taking vegetation concentrates that made her hair grow long and silky soft. More than anything else, she wanted to be a television star.

Because of satellites from the misty blue planet called "Earth," Drucanites had been watching television programs for fifteen years, longer than Laddru's life. They couldn't understand the strange languages they heard very well, especially since the misty planet had several languages that changed with just a slight variation in a satellite's rotation. Laddru, though, worked hard at understanding the language of a space drama called "Star Trek." It was the same language the astronauts spoke.

It used to be a dream. Now it was a necessity, all because of Unfrey, the boy she hated most because he hated her white hair. Jealous creep. He got all the others teasing her, too. They ganged up on her yesterday after school, shouting. "We know what you're taking."

"Do not."

"Yes, we do. You're taking ambloids to make your fur white."

"So what if I am."

Unfrey taunted, "She says she's going to be a star on television. How you getting to Earth, huh?"

"I'm going, just you wait."

"She won't go," one of the others said.

"I'll jetpack to their satellite," Laddru replied.

Unfrey sneered. "You wouldn't dare."

"Yeah," the others shouted. "We dare you."

Laddru shouted back, "I'll take your dare and prove it."

Willing Suspension of Disbelief *(cont.)*

Laddru's Dare (cont.)

Thoughts, Questions

They made her swear on the dreams of Mui—whom Earthlings called God—that she'd go. That did it. Now she had to go.

Luckily, she'd been studying the makeup of Earth's atmosphere. Drucan's atmosphere was similar to that of Mars, even though it was far closer to the Earth's moon than to Mars.

She devised a way to survive Earth's atmosphere through a slow build up of medication she'd made from Drucan toads. She'd been taking it for two years now, and knew that it, along with her hair, would protect her cells from the cold of space and any strange atmosphere.

As her father spoke on and on about values and growing up, Laddru thought of a way to add enough fuel to her jetpack to make it all the way out to a satellite.

A few days after her birthday, she heard that a satellite from Earth had entered into Drucan's orbit and a spaceship from Earth would be looking for it. It was now or never. Greatly excited, she lied to her best friend, saying her fuel pack leaked so she could borrow her friend's. Now, with two fuel packs she was ready to jump to the satellite as soon as it came into view.

Laddru knew the undertaking would be dangerous, that her mother would be furious, and her father . . . she couldn't even imagine what he'd do. Still, the dare pulled her. She wrote a note to her mother, telling her not to worry and to watch for her on television. As soon as she saw the satellite, she put the note in her mother's flower bowl, activated the electronic force field to keep her warm, and shot straight up.

She had to make a couple of passes before she caught the edge of the satellite, but she made it, suspecting that in the process she knocked out all the television screens on Drucan.

Name _____ Date _____

Willing Suspension of Disbelief *(cont.)*

Laddru's Dare (cont.)

Now what? Despite the force field and her thick hair, it was mighty cold sitting on that big metal disc. Nevertheless, she strapped herself onto the satellite and waited to see what would happen next. Thank Mui, she thought, for my white, silky hair. As her jetpack fell into Drucan's orbit, she noticed the satellite was pulling out of it. Her heart raced with excitement.

Suddenly she felt a sharp jerk, and the satellite went into free fall. What fun! After a while it settled into a soft float. She could hear the strange languages bouncing off the satellite and knew she'd fallen into Earth's orbit.

Soon she saw the spaceship moving very slowly towards her. She recognized it from their television news. They were coming to the satellite to repair something. She studied the satellite; noticed a small, square metal box dangling from a single wire.

As the spaceship approached, she began combing her hair with her fingers, fluffing it. She unleashed herself and hid as best she could beneath the satellite.

Two funny looking Earthlings floated out of an opening in the ship. They were big and tall— almost two meters tall. They had to wear those protective spacesuits because they didn't know how to use electronic force fields and atmospheric medications. Maybe she could teach them.

They floated toward her but luckily didn't see her, concentrating instead on re-plugging the metal box into one side of the satellite. While they worked, she jumped into the space ship. The Earthling at the console inside didn't see her, either.

Thoughts, Questions

_____
_____
_____
_____
_____
_____
_____
_____
_____
_____
_____
_____
_____
_____
_____
_____
_____
_____
_____
_____
_____
_____
_____
_____
_____
_____

Name _____ Date _____

Willing Suspension of Disbelief (cont.)

Laddru's Dare (cont.)

Thoughts, Questions

She hid behind a strange protrusion, hung onto a metal bar, and thought with pride, I'm a stowaway. She could hardly wait to get on television and wave to Unfrey and his stupid friends. They wouldn't ever tease her again.

After a couple of hours, the astronauts returned to the ship and latched the door closed. The last one in said, "Mission accomplished." He took off his helmet, revealing a head full of curly red hair and bright blue eyes.

The other had blue eyes, too, but with a hint of green. He held up his fingers, his thumb and forefinger forming a circle. All three astronauts were grinning.

Laddru forgot herself and let go of the bar she'd been holding. She floated out in full view.

The pinkish faces of two of the Earthlings turned as white as her fur. The face of the one at the controls was a very pretty brown, and it didn't change color. "My God, what's that?" he asked.

"Easy, Matt," one said. "Just watch it."

Matt started talking into a microphone. His voice was high pitched—full of fear. Laddru wondered what he was afraid of. She looked him over and felt kind and gentle toward him.

"Man oh man, Donahue, look at those eyes," the other astronaut said.

She wanted to say something, but couldn't quite get her tongue around the sounds of their language. From television she'd learned to understand pretty much what these astronauts were saying, but didn't feel confident to speak.

The one called Donahue said, "They're absolutely beautiful. Soft. Like eyes on a Pekinese. And get a load of that hair. It shines."

Laddru liked these critters and floated over to them. The one called Matt reached out as if he wanted to touch her but didn't dare.

Name _____ Date _____

Willing Suspension of Disbelief *(cont.)*

Laddru's Dare (cont.)

"Wow. What hair. Man, that looks soft."

"It's almost iridescent," Donahue said in a reverent tone.

Loud, irritating static invaded the spacecraft.

Matt, at the controls, spoke rapidly into the microphone, looking over at Laddru all the while.

She was so glad she'd come!

Donahue reached out and began stroking her back. It was a strange sensation, but she enjoyed it. It made her very sleepy. Then he stopped to float around the cabin while they drank something through a long, narrow tube. Donahue offered her a sip from what he said was his "straw." She was feeling a little hungry, but wasn't sure how to use it.

Embarrassed, she ducked her head for a second and floated away from Donahue.

"Look at that," he said. "It's shy."

"I'm not an it," she wanted to say, "I'm a Drucan woman, full grown."

After a while, hunger got the best of her.

Besides, she'd watched them inhale through those tubes long enough to figure she could do it, too. She floated toward her astronaut and made sucking motions with her lips.

He let out funny little noises and handed her his drink. The other two grinned.

She inhaled a thick white goo that tasted ordinary, neither good nor bad. But it did ease her hunger pangs. She looked at each of them as she sucked on the straw. They were all staring at her so hard that they sometimes bumped into each other as they floated around the cabin.

In a gruff voice, Matt said, "Prepare for landing."

Thoughts, Questions

_____
_____
_____
_____
_____
_____
_____
_____
_____
_____
_____
_____
_____
_____
_____
_____
_____
_____
_____
_____
_____
_____
_____

Name _____ Date _____

Willing Suspension of Disbelief *(cont.)*

Laddru's Dare (cont.)   **Thoughts, Questions**

The astronauts belted themselves to metal slabs.

Donahue reached out, pulled her to him, and held her tight.

A loud explosion was followed by a terrific shudder, a whoosh, and a hard jolt.

"We made it," Matt shouted.

"Wait until the reporters see this," Donahue said. "We'll be lucky to get it through debriefing."

Soon the door opened. Laddru felt a rush of pressure as if something were pushing her onto the ground. She grabbed her astronaut's hand and implored him with her eyes.

"It's okay, Buddy," he said. "Don't worry, it's just Earth's gravity. You'll get used to it."

She tried to stand, slowly stretched to her full sixty-six centimeters, and brushed her hair with her fingertips.

Peeking out the door, she saw a crowd of Earthlings without any spacesuits on. Their bodies were wrapped in more shades of color than she'd ever seen. Pretty, she thought.

Struggling against the weight of the air, she moved out the door so they could see her. This is it! The misty blue planet.

Three big, black boxes with round eyes moved towards her. She heard someone shout, "Watch out for the Channel Seven camera."

Television. They were filming her. She waved at the machine and called out in Drucan, "Hi, Mom and Dad. See, I made it to Earth. I'm gonna be a regular on your television. I love you." It pleased her to ignore Unfrey.

She started down the gangplank when someone in a white coat picked her up and shoved her into a screen covered box. She was trapped! She swore in Drucan at the white-coat and called out for her astronaut.

Name _____ Date _____

Willing Suspension of Disbelief (cont.)

Laddru's Dare (cont.)

Thoughts, Questions

He ran over to her and said, "I'm so sorry, little Buddy. They have to run tests on you. I'm so sorry." There were tears in his eyes when he turned away.

Some horrible Earthling shoved a needle into her shoulder. She shuddered and the world went black.

◆ ◆ ◆ ◆

When Laddru woke up she was still in the cage, but it sat in the middle of a huge empty room that echoed her voice when she spoke. Through a high window she could see the sky just beginning to turn pink. Inside the cage was a bowl of water and a dish with little round pebbles in it. Ugly brown balls. She tasted one. It was so foul tasting she spit it out and drank the water. It, too, had a strange metallic taste.

Her shoulder hurt from the shot. She felt so alone and miserable, she wished she'd never left home. Tears started to wet her cheeks. She choked them off and looked for a way to escape.

Searching the cage, she found a spot where the metal looked a little weak. She started chewing the wire. After five minutes she'd chewed a hole big enough to tear open. Soon she was out of the cage. The window was open. She made a running jump and landed on the window sill. She nearly cried again when she found another metal screen.

Choking back her tears, she began chewing. Mui, it was foul tasting! Almost as bad as the brown balls.

She made it through the window and jumped down to a sidewalk. By now the sky was a hazy blue. She tried to get used to the shock of noisy cars that whizzed by so fast they blurred together. They smelled awful. She longed for her sweet smelling jetpack. After a few moments she realized one of those stinky cars could kill her if she got in its way.

Name _____ Date _____

Willing Suspension of Disbelief (cont.)

Laddru's Dare (cont.)

Besides, whenever a driver spotted her he did something to make his car squeal and go every which way.

Keeping close to the buildings, she moved down the sidewalk. A dog growled at her and pawed the ground.

Frightened, she moved faster. Soon a whole pack of dogs started following her. She ran. They kept up with her, barking. One dog, twice her size, tried to bite her. Panicked, she jumped as high as she could and landed on top of a gold painted sign, one she recognized from television commercials.

Inside they sold hamburgers and what Earthlings called "fries." Little Earthlings about her size played in a cage full of brightly colored balls.

The dogs barked at her until a big Earthling shooed them away. What a relief. She was sliding down the sign when she felt someone pick her up by the back of her neck. That hurt. She yelped.

"What the heck are you?" a deep and scratchy-voiced Earthling asked. He felt her hair. "Now, wouldn't that make a nice weaving?" He carried her by her neck down a street to a room full of mirrors and tall chairs. A sign over the door said "Barber Shop."

The next thing she knew, she was sitting on one of the chairs. Another white-coated Earthling was running a machine down her back. Oh no! They were shaving off her lovely white hair! She struggled, but both of these awful critters held her down.

Finally she was able to twist her neck around and give one critter's hand a quick bite—restrained. (A hard one would snap his hand off!) He yelled and let go. She snapped her teeth at the other one, and he let go, too. With a big jump she escaped out the door and started running. If only she could find Donahue!

Thoughts, Questions

_____

_____

_____

_____

_____

_____

_____

_____

_____

_____

_____

_____

_____

_____

_____

_____

_____

_____

_____

_____

_____

_____

_____

Name _____ Date _____

Willing Suspension of Disbelief *(cont.)*

Laddru's Dare (cont.)

Thoughts, Questions

When she ran out of breath, she stopped.

Panting, she surveyed her surroundings. Across the street she saw a grassy area with lots of big flowering bushes and trees. If she could get over there, she could hide in the bushes until her hair grew back. While waiting for the traffic to clear, she looked up and caught a glimpse of herself in a mirror on a high pole. What a shock! Without her hair she looked like some wild creature from outer space.

Her translucent skin showed her pounding heart.

And her hair might not grow back white unless the medicine was still in her system.

The traffic cleared, and she ran across the street.

Hiding in the bushes, she heard a siren. Then she saw several black and white cars with flashing red lights go by at top speed. Were they looking for her?

Oh, Mama, she cried to herself, why did I think they'd be nice to me here? Is this what you meant, Dad, about growing up?

For fifteen revolutions around the sun she hid in the park, waiting for her hair to grow. She dug a hole under an oleander bush and there she lived, sleeping during the day, foraging for food at night. She had several close calls, but no one caught her.

She longed for a home. She'd seen plenty of homes on television, millions of them in this city they called L.A., wherever it was. Certainly, if she were anywhere near Drucan, she'd go home.

One night she came out of an alley with a bag of oranges she'd found there. Suddenly it started raining. At first she thought someone was pouring water on her. Soon she realized it was coming from the sky. She'd read about rain, but had never felt it.

It had a nice metallic smell and washed her clean.

She looked down at the white fuzz growing back. At least it was still white.

Name _____ Date _____

Willing Suspension of Disbelief (cont.)

Laddru's Dare (cont.)

Some television sets were playing in a store window. Since nobody was around, she chanced a watch. After all, she hadn't seen any news for a long time.

To her amazement, she saw her old, long-haired self on the screen as she got off the spaceship with her astronaut. If only she knew where he lived.

He'd help her. The newscaster was saying, "Astronaut Donahue is offering a reward for the return of this little Drucan. The last sighting was at a barber shop on Sepulveda Boulevard where it bit the barber and ran away. Evidently it can jump quite high."

Laddru felt a thrill run through her. He was looking for her! Then she was overcome with sorrow for her parents who undoubtedly watched this very program. To think she used to feel lonely.

Nothing compared to the loneliness she felt now.

Whom could she trust? At least she knew her astronaut's name. She tried saying it aloud, but she knew her voice didn't sound anything like an Earthling's. Finally, she worked up enough courage to enter the store.

A bell rang when she pushed open the door. A man's voice called, "We're closing now. Come back tomorrow."

"Ast-ro-naut Don-a-hoo," she said as loudly as she could. The words were right, but somehow she couldn't get the inflection.

"Who's there?" the man asked. He picked up a gun and moved toward her. His shoulders leaned forward, and he didn't have any hair except around his ears. She wondered why he had shaved his head. Since he was looking up and out the door, he didn't see her.

Thoughts, Questions

_____

_____

_____

_____

_____

_____

_____

_____

_____

_____

_____

_____

_____

_____

_____

_____

_____

_____

_____

_____

_____

_____

_____

_____

Name _____ Date _____

Willing Suspension of Disbelief (cont.)

Laddru's Dare (cont.)	**Thoughts, Questions**

When he stood two feet away, she repeated, "Ast-ro-naut Don-a-hoo."

He swung the gun in her direction. "Where are you?"

"Here," she replied, proud she knew how to speak.

He looked down and screamed. Did she look that bad?

She backed toward the door, clutching the bag of oranges to her chest.

He pointed the gun at her. "What are you?"

"Ast-ro-naut Don-a-hoo," she repeated. "Shoot not."

Suddenly, he understood. "You're the little Drucan. Stay right there. I'll get the astronaut for you."

Laddru watched him lock the front door and then back up to a counter, watching her all the while.

How could he be afraid of her?

He punched a black machine with his fingers and then talked into a handle he held in his hand. She heard sirens coming, that same mournful sound she'd heard so often since she'd gone to live under the oleander bush.

Soon the man brought the black machine toward her and beckoned for her to come listen. Timidly she moved forward. He held the handle to her ear. She heard her astronaut say, "Hey little Buddy, say something. Let me know I've found you."

"Ast-ro-naut Don-a-hoo."

"It's you! It's you," he shouted. "Stay there. I'll be there in ten minutes."

Laddru dropped the bag of oranges and smiled.

The shaved Earthling smiled back. She tried to fluff her hair, but it was still too short. At least it had grown enough to hide her beating heart.

Willing Suspension of Disbelief *(cont.)*

Laddru's Dare (cont.)

Some critters in black uniforms banged on the door. The shaved one let them in. They stood around staring at her, but kept their guns in some kind of cases at their waists.

Pretty soon her astronaut arrived. He swooped her up into his arms and held her tight. "My poor little buddy. How could they shave off your beautiful hair? We've gotta get you home, somehow. Any idea how?"

"Television," Laddru said. "Drucans watch."

"They watch our TV?"

"Satellite. Take me to satellite. Say to Drucans send jetpack. Home." She buried her face in his neck.

As he carried her to a car, he said, "You're very famous, do you know that?"

"Fame important no more," she answered. "Hair not value. Home value."

"Well, aren't you the grown up little thing!"

"Grown up? No. But I won't make dare again."

"We'll get you home," he said, and she knew he would.

Thoughts, Questions

_____

_____

_____

_____

_____

_____

_____

_____

_____

_____

_____

_____

_____

What are the major themes of this story?

_____

_____

_____

Were they explicit (directly stated) or implicit (implied)?

_____

_____

Now read the story again as a scientist. Return to your disbelief. A science fiction story may have all kinds of incredible things happening in it, but the science must be credible.

What are the scientific flaws in this story? Go back to your margin notes and add to your comments from your first reading.

Writing Science Fiction

Now it is your turn. With a partner, by yourself, or with your group, write your own science fiction story. What are you studying in science this semester that you can use as a launching pad for a short story?

As you think about that for a few days, consider also what you need to invent for your story.

The major elements of a short story are these: *character, plot, setting, theme.* If you begin at the top of the abstraction ladder with theme, you will have trouble writing. Fiction starts at the very bottom of the ladder.

You may want to start with character. In that case, brainstorm the following: *name, age, physical characteristics, burning desires, personality traits, flaws, skills.*

You may want to start with plot. What are the stakes? What is the major conflict? Why are the characters acting like fools one moment and heroes the next? (If they are, that is.) Look back at E.M. Forster's definition of plot.

Once you have decided on characters and plot, make an operational analysis of your story, scene by scene. A scene contains description of the setting, description of the characters as they are introduced, and dialogue that reveals what the main character wants and who or what is thwarting the character.

Your main character may be a creature on Jupiter who came to life after the comet fragments struck that planet or a creature who crawled up from the molten core of the Earth. The creature—he, she, or it—wants something badly.

To make your sci-fi believable, even though your characters are not, you must fill in the details of the setting as honestly and truly as you can. Use your imagination freely, but ground it in solid scientific facts.

The truer you are to nature, human and otherwise, the more bizarre you can be with setting and characters.

There are seven basic plots in all storytelling. You do not need to know them to write a good story. You simply need to know that the concrete details you select to show your characters in conflict should be specimens only. For example, notice the specific information in the following passage:

She twisted the gold chain of her necklace as she spoke. The blue teardrop pendant dropped off and hit the marble tile with an echoing chime. Her host gasped. "The marble!" he shouted. "Watch out. Now it'll burn you."

Write on.

Growth in Artistic Expression

This section echoes some of the information and procedures of the other disciplines and adds art specific lessons. Placing students in small groups may be difficult for the actual making of art. The small group interaction, however, works best for content learning. Some learning calls for partnership interaction, some for two-team competition as in the old spelling bee (in this case, the vocabulary special to art). Artistic expression involves thinking, writing, science, math, history, and technology; therefore, each is included, indirectly if not directly.

Since this supplemental text cannot carry reprints of works under discussion, it refers to works that are famous enough to be found in your school or district library. The suggested activities here are predominantly reading, writing, and drawing because the materials are readily available and the practice invaluable.

A pretest of sorts is suggested, a timed drawing of a Halloween mask. This, too, is arbitrary and subject to your change.

The most important concept for students to learn is the fact that *words change meaning as they change context*, that each discipline uses general words in context-specific ways. (Have you ever tried to read a computer manual and asked, "What do they mean by *script*? Or *protocol*?") Therefore, this section opens after a brief pretest, with the vocabulary for learning the language of art followed by a passage on the significance and history of artistic expression. You may wish to read small portions of this aloud to the class daily as they draw or have the students read, discuss, and paraphrase in small groups. Undoubtedly, the attention span of your students will direct your choices.

Portfolio assessment allows you to grade students on multiple talents and on the extent of their participation in the learning process. Pages calling for student name and date are included here for portfolio collections.

Name _____ Date _____

Artistic Expression

If you have ever seen ancient symbols and drawings on the sandstone walls of cliffs and caves, you may have been stimulated to think of contemporary graffiti spray-painted on city walls or of civic signs and logos in many cities of the world.

From your studies in science, do you remember the following rather hefty quotation from William James? Read it again and apply it to art:

> *Man's chief differences from the brutes lies in the exuberant excess of his subjective propensities. His preeminence over them lies simply and solely in the number and in the fantastic and unnecessary character of his wants—physical, moral, aesthetic and intellectual. Had his whole life not been a quest for the superfluous, he would never have established himself so inexpungeably in the necessary. And from the consciousness of this, he should draw the lesson that his wants are to be trusted, that even when their gratification seems furthest off, the uneasiness they occasion is still the best guide of his life, and will lead him to issues entirely beyond his present powers of reckoning. Prune down his extravagances, sober him, and you undo him.*

Artistic expression is one of man's subjective propensities, a quest for the superfluous, the unnecessary.

Name _____ Date _____

Artistic Expression *(cont.)*

What is the difference between graffiti and art? Between a painting in a museum of contemporary art that looks like a bunch of lines on a huge canvas and the crayon drawings your kid sister makes in kindergarten? What does it all mean?

In this section we will, together, make several attempts to answer that question and have fun creating some art at the same time.

If you have ever said to anyone, "I can't draw," it was a mistake, an innocent lie. Everyone can draw— maybe not as well as Michelangelo or Picasso, but everyone can draw. You can and so can your kid sister.

In the space below, make a line drawing of your favorite Halloween mask. Put it in your portfolio. At the end of the course, draw another one so you can compare them and see your progress in technique as well as aesthetic sensibility.

Name _____ Date _____

The Language of Art

Aesthetic sensibility is the degree to which you are tuned in to beauty and to its conditions, the degree to which you are aware of its principles—the concepts that help us define beauty. Aesthetic perception refers to learning to see the world metaphorically as well as directly. For example, a gun is a weapon for killing. It is also a symbol of brute power.

Aesthetic experience is an experience that you value for its sake alone. It can do nothing for you except please you for the duration of the experience. While it lasts, you are aware of the relationship between the form and content of the experience.

Have you ever heard anyone say, "I don't know much about art, but I know what I like"? The aesthetic experience is enhanced when you do know much about art, for in the knowing you become aware of principles of beauty and the relationship between form and content.

The following glossary of basic terms is printed on one side of your page so you can write, paraphrase, and draw the meaning of each term as it is used in visual art. Do not leave the space blank, for in responding to the terms, you learn to use them.

Basic Terms

Color is made up of hue, value, and intensity. When you see a color, your sensation depends on the reflection or absorption of light from a given surface.

Hue is determined by the specific wave length of the color in the ray of light. Every ray of light coming from the sun is composed of waves which vibrate at different speeds. The sensation of color which humans experience comes from the way our vision responds to different wave lengths. If a light beam passes through a triangular piece of glass (prism) onto a sheet of white paper, the rays of light will bend at different angles as they pass through the glass and will show up on the paper as color. Hue tells us the color's position in the spectrum.

Question, Paraphrase, Draw

Name _____ Date _____

The Language of Art *(cont.)*

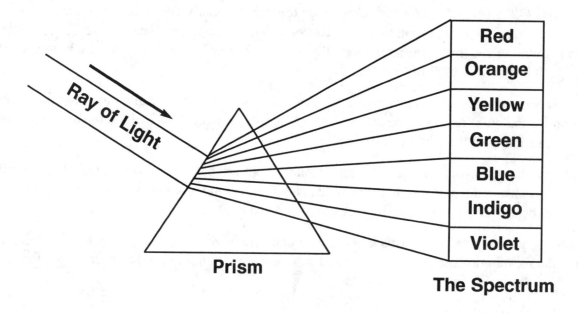

Prism

The Spectrum

Basic Terms

Value: the gradation of light and dark. It refers to the lightness or darkness of tone, the quantity of light, not the quality. In mixing colors we can produce a wide variety of tones by adding neutrals, black, or white.

Intensity: the saturation or strength of a color determined by the quality of light reflected from it. A vivid color is of high intensity. In the bright sunlight of the tropics, colors are intense. In the diffused light of northern climates, colors are less intense.

Analogous colors: those colors are closely related in hue, for analogies show relationships.

Question, Paraphrase, Draw

116

Name _____ Date _____

The Language of Art *(cont.)*

Basic Terms

Color Tonality: color schemes including the three aspects of color— hue, value, and intensity.

Line: an identifiable path of a point moving in space.

Shape: a two-dimensional area or plane that may be organic or inorganic, free-form or geometric, open or closed, natural or of human origin.

Form: a three-dimensional (or possessing the illusion of three dimensions) volume with the same qualities as shape. (Remember that volume has a lot more meanings than what you turn up for more sound.)

Form (another definition): the totality of the work of art; the organization (design) of all elements which make up the work; elements of form—line, shapes, values, textures, and colors.

Volume: any three-dimensional quantity that is bound or enclosed, whether solid or void.

Space: a volume available for occupation by form; an extent, measurable or infinite, that can be understood as an area or distance, one capable of being used negatively and positively.

Mass: the actual or implied physical bulk, weight, and density of three-dimensional forms occupying real or suggested spatial depth. How do you define mass in your science class?

Question, Paraphrase, Draw

The Language of Art *(cont.)*

Basic Terms

Texture: the surface quality of materials, either actual or visual.

Media, Medium: the materials and tools used by the artist.

Technique: the manner and skill with which the artist uses tools and materials—the ways that use of media affects aesthetic quality.

Representation: subject matter naturally presented; visual elements which look like actual forms.

Naturalism: all forms used by the artist appearing essentially representative.

Abstract, Abstraction: forms created by the artist abstracted, or "pulled out," from real objects; the essence of something. (There may be little or no resemblance to the original object.)

Balance: an equilibrium of similar, opposing, or contrasting elements that together create a unity.

Symmetry: a balance in which elements are alike and will appear to demand one another.

Asymmetry: a balance achieved through the use of unequal parts or elements.

Contrast: use of opposites in close proximity (light and dark, rough and smooth).

Question, Paraphrase, Draw

Name _____ Date _____

The Language of Art *(cont.)*

Basic Terms

Dominance: the difference in importance of one aspect in relation to all other aspects.

Repetition: the recurrence of elements at regular intervals.

Rhythm: the regular repetition of particular forms or stresses and the suggestion of motion by recurrent forms.

Style: individual mode of expression and, in its genus, a family of characteristics when applied to a period of time or particular school of art.

Content (or form-meaning): the final statement, mood, or spectator experience with a work of art; the significance of the art form.

Question, Paraphrase, Draw

Art Vocabulary Bee

1. Because your understanding of the words your teachers use in any field of learning has a direct effect on what or whether you learn, take a look now at your questions, drawings, or paraphrases and compare what you have with other members of your group. Discuss the meaning of each term. Come up with examples for each.

2. You can make a word yours for life if you use it three times—twice in speaking and once in writing. Take some time to use the art terms in meaningful ways in your speech and in another way in a written sentence.

3. Divide your class in two. Line up on both sides of the room. Appoint a scorekeeper. Have members of each team draw basic terms from a hat and attempt to explain them. Let your teacher be the final judge on whether or not you came close enough to stay in line.

A Bit of History

Like a writer, musician, architect, cartoonist, or movie director, the visual artist expresses his perceptions of his time. The history of art parallels the history of technology in most interesting ways.

The Relationship of Technology to Art

◆ In the 18th century the machine—any kind of machine—was exotic.

◆ By the 19th century, the machine was still new to social experiences.

◆ By the 20th century, the machine was a cliché, no longer considered for artistic expression.

In 1850, most of the world was rural. People lived in the country or in small villages. By 1900 the machine had centralized process and product and tipped the balance of population toward cities.

Artistic expression moved from pastoral images of nature to images of city life. In the country, things grow; the essence of the city is manufacture or process, and this could be expressed artistically only by metaphors of linkage, relativity, and interconnectedness.

The rate of change in technology in the 19th century was so fast it left art stranded for a while in rural images. Conventional paintings could not deal with the new experience of fast travel in a machine on wheels. The machine meant the conquest of horizontal space and the succession and superimposition of views. Landscapes unfolded in flickering surfaces. The view from the train was not the view from the horse. It compressed motifs and left less time to dwell on any one thing. These fast-moving images could not be captured, at least before the movie camera was invented.

Also, representational art was replaced by the photograph. The speed at which culture reinvented itself through technology during the last quarter of the 19th century and the first of the 20th seemed almost in opposition to nature. Consider these inventions:

◆ phonograph　　　　　　◆ light bulb

◆ X-rays　　　　　　◆ machine gun

◆ steam turbine　　　　　　◆ synthetic fiber

◆ telegraph　　　　　　◆ photographic paper

◆ automobile　　　　　　◆ airplane

◆ camera　　　　　　◆ movie camera

A Bit of History *(cont.)*

As the age of steam passed into the age of electricity, the sense of an accelerated rate of change affected all areas of human endeavor, including art.

Technology changed man's view of himself and the world. Artists had the problem of making paintings and sculpture that would reflect these changes in consciousness.

The question then became this: *How, by slowly shoving paint across a canvas, could an artist produce a convincing record of speeding processes and change?*

The first artists to answer this were the Cubists. Cubism was the first radically new proposal about how we see; in fact, it was the first radical new proposal that painting had made in five hundred years.

Since the Renaissance, almost all painting has obeyed the convention of one-point perspective, a geometrical system for depicting the illusion of reality. Once the construction for setting up a perspective scene is known, things can be represented on a flat sheet of paper as though they were in space.

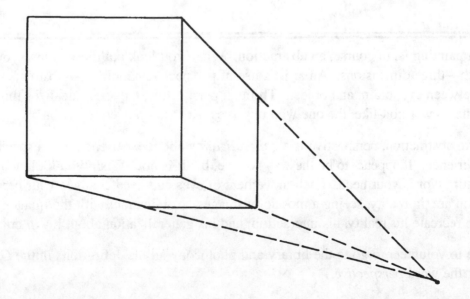

Name _____ Date _____

A Bit of History *(cont.)*

Perspective in the 15th century was seen not only as a branch of mathematics but also as magic. Imagine the magic of finding the same perspective with the click of a camera button. Look around you now. Find an example of one-point perspective and draw it below.

Perspective in painting is, of course, an abstraction. When you look out the window, your eyes and brain see depth—three dimensions. An artist's use of perspective simplifies—abstracts—the relationship between eye, brain, and object. Through perspective, the artist idealizes this relationship, thus making the viewer god-like, the one who observes but is not moved to action.

Because it is an abstraction, perspective is a *generalization* about experience, not a specific rendering of a specific experience. It appears to be the way we see, but it is not. When you look at an object, your eye is never still. Nor is your head. Each movement of eyes and head changes your perspective, if only minimally. You are, in reality, seeing a mosaic of images. You interact with the images you see. The painter tries to recreate his reality, his interaction, and his generalization about his interactions.

(Ask someone to volunteer to go to the library and photocopy all the definitions in the *Oxford English Dictionary* for the word *perspective*.)

A Bit of History *(cont.)*

Compare the thought about interaction with what you learn in writing: the reader and the writer should be as metaphorically close as the pencil that separates them.

Try this experiment on multiple perspectives now. Hold an object in your hand. Study it for three minutes. Try to hold still. How many different glimpses do you have of that object?

In your study of science you encountered the idea that the viewer, by watching, affects what is being watched. (Remember the comparison between the light which scientists use to see the interior of a cell with a fire hose turned on a classroom full of students?)

This concept is found in art, also. It does not mean that everything is subjective. Nor does it mean that if we see a spider under the chair we can will the creature out of existence as a figment of our imagination. It does mean our close presence may influence the spider, much as a classroom observer from the outside influences your behavior in the classroom.

It also means our perception of the spider is colored by everything we know about spiders and our experience with them. In other words, our eyes and the objects we see influence one another mutually and reciprocally. In the late 19th century this was not generally thought to be true. In the early 20th century the idea developed in the works of Alfred North Whitehead in philosophy, Albert Einstein in physics, and, unaware of their works, Paul Cezanne in painting.

In 1906, just before he died, Cezanne wrote that he was growing more clear-sighted looking at nature but realized that he could never attain the intensity nor richness of color that animates nature. On the banks of the river he studied, he said the motifs multiplied.

These "motifs," a word common to music, were the relationships between grass and rock, tree and shadow, leaf and cloud, which blossomed into an infinity of small truths each time Cezanne moved his head.

Name _____ Date _____

A Bit of History *(cont.)*

Multiple Perspectives

1. In space one below, draw a quick sketch of the object you recently held for three minutes.

2. Now look at the object again and draw it again in space two.

3. Look at it from a slightly different angle and draw it again in space three.

4. Repeat all three drawings in space four, this time overlapping the drawings. Can you see all three as a design worth coloring?

1	2	3

4

Name _____ Date _____

A Bit of History *(cont.)*

Pablo Picasso

How sure are you of what you see when you look at something?

Picasso and other cubists wanted to represent the fact that knowledge of an object is made up of all possible views of it—top, sides, front, and back. They wanted to compress these views into one moment, one synthesized view, as you just did with your object.

After five hundred years of one-point perspective, the cubists made war on it, and relative size was one of the first casualties. An eye could be twice as big as a hand, for example, depending on what the artist wanted to convey.

Picasso based his art on physical sensation. He had an amazing ability to make his viewers feel the shape, the weight, the edginess, and the silence of things.

Close your eyes long enough to imagine you can feel the shape, the weight, the edginess, and the silence of a dead bird. Draw it below in its silence.

Name _____ Date _____

A Bit of History *(cont.)*

As Picasso moved toward abstraction, he conceived of sculpture not as a solid mass, but as an open construction of planes. In painting he would include just enough signs of the real world to supply a tension between reality outside the painting and the visual language inside.

In some of his paintings, reality vanished. The viewer has to imagine the world of his paintings as a network of fleeting events. When you see a fish swimming in a pond, you do not see the whole fish, you see shimmers of its back in the water and imagine the fish. Imagine, then, a painting of this fish.

Picasso, though, denied he was an abstract painter. He said, "I paint forms as I think them, not as I see them."

Try that now with your object. Hold it in front of you and think about it. Draw it as you think of it, not as you see it.

Name _____ Date _____

A Bit of History *(cont.)*

Abstract art has been with us for 80 years now. Artists have played with forms that promote a feeling of uneasiness, a hint of something just on the edge of our awareness. These forms are metaphors for 20th century angst (free-floating worry).

Imagine two television sets facing each other and broadcasting two different talk shows. Would you call it "Dialogue" or "I'm Listening"?

Imagine a store with a huge display of television sets of all shapes and sizes showing an exploding airplane. Would you feel comfortable in such a store?

Think of some of the horrible images you have seen on television or in the movies and have deposited in your mental picture bank. Close your eyes for a moment and let the images come back to you.

Try drawing one of them below in abstract. In other words, remove the horror without denying it.

Painting, along with everything else we humans do, creates a sense of wholeness, makes order out of chaos. Painting does not pretend things are whole when they are not. It makes visible the opposition between order and chaos.

(As in literature, the rendition must carry the *artist's truth*; it must not be slanted toward the imagined tastes of a mass audience.)

Name _____ Date _____

A Bit of History *(cont.)*

Consider the following two statements. Discuss their meanings in your group or with a partner. Paraphrase each one in your own words.

1. *No painting is wholly abstract. All art, in some way or another is situated in this world, hoping to act as a transformer between the self and the non-self.*

   Paraphrase: _____

   _____

   _____

   _____

   _____

   _____

   _____

   _____

2. *Art discovers its true social use by opening the passageway from feeling to meaning.*

   Paraphrase: _____

   _____

   _____

   _____

   _____

   _____

   _____

Postscript on Picasso: There are negative features to fame, but one positive feature for Picasso was his famous signature. Because of its unique form and his fame, no one would cash his checks, keeping them instead as souvenir autographs. Therefore, he wrote checks for everything, but his money stayed in his bank account.

128

Name _____ Date _____

Ways of Seeing

The story of art is the story of seeing. The visual artist leads our seeing, shows us how to see excitement in the ordinary, beauty in the ugly, and the sometimes ugly aspects of beauty. When you create art, you are seeing more than you normally do.

Once you see something, you cannot *not* see it. For example, in Australia one American looked up at the full moon and saw a clear outline of a rabbit. She had never noticed a rabbit in the moon before. Later she learned that in those parts of the world where the rabbit is obvious, mythology contains several references to the hare in the moon.

When she returned to the northern hemisphere, she had to tilt her head to the right to see the rabbit. Each month now, looking straight up, she sees a man or woman's face. However, she still sees the rabbit, too.

Pick up your object now and look at it with your head tilted far to the right. Hold it upside down. Let it speak to you. What does it say?

_____

_____

_____

What new things do you see?

_____

_____

_____

Imagine for a moment that you are feeling very sad or very happy or very angry. Hold the feeling and look at your object. Does it look the same? Draw it here from the perspective of your feeling.

Name _____ Date _____

Ways of Seeing (cont.)

People speak of *poetic vision*. How do you see that phrase? What does it mean to you?

_____

_____

_____

_____

_____

_____

In the first section of this text, we discussed the abstraction ladder, noting that it is easier to see how things are different than how they are alike. But, if we put these things on a ladder or on a classification, structural, or operational diagram, we see how they are related.

If we are going to really see, we must see things in relationships. Picasso saw how the things he drew, sculpted, and painted related to other aspects of his world and other works of art. We could say he had "poetic vision." (He well may not have said that about himself.)

Pick up your object. Look at it in relation to other things in your world, to works of art you can see now, to music you have heard, stories you have read, or games you have played. Place it on a rung of an abstraction ladder with any of these things above and below it.

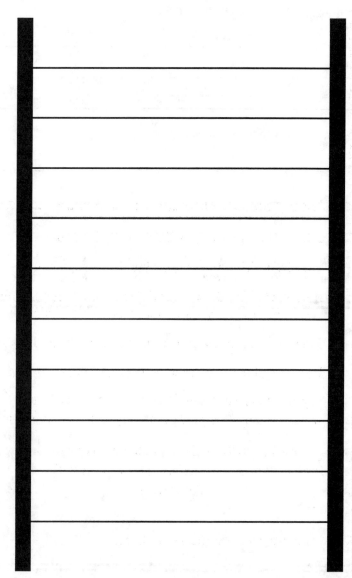

130

Name _____ Date _____

Ways of Seeing *(cont.)*

Now draw your object again as you think of it in relation to other things on your abstraction ladder.

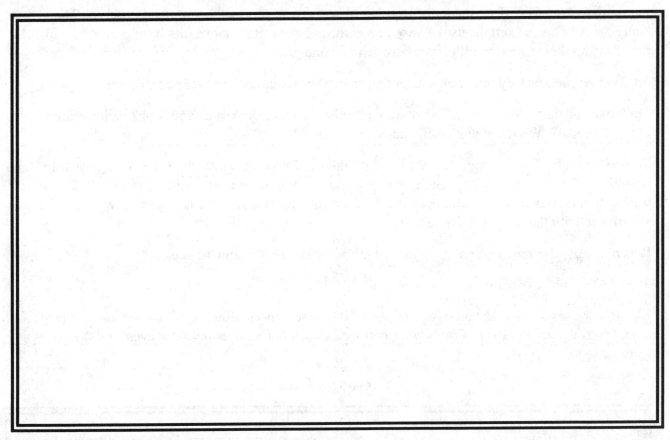

We have looked at four approaches to artistic expression:

1. **Realistic:** You drew your object as you saw it.

2. **Abstract:** You drew your object from different angles and layered the perspectives. Perhaps you were able to convey a message or find a design.

3. **Feeling:** You drew your object to express an intense feeling.

4. **Poetic vision:** You drew your object in relation to other things in your world.

You may not have succeeded at any of these, at least to your satisfaction. But so what? You explored. Now we are going to explore drawing with all five senses.

As you recall from your English classes, your job as a writer is to select concrete material from your environment and put it together on the page, either for a chosen reason or to discover what you can or cannot do with it. (The concrete used to make sidewalks is *not* what is meant here. What concrete is meant?)

A visual artist must do the same thing.

Name _____ Date _____

Ways of Seeing *(cont.)*

Practices in Drawing

Learning to draw is really a matter of learning to see. To see correctly, you must observe. The phrase "nitty gritty" comes from the use of very fine combs or sieves to remove nits from corn grits. Imagine the effort it takes to see the difference between nits and grits.

To observe you must try to use as many of your five senses at once as you possibly can.

Look once again at your object. What are your other senses aware of as you look? What does your object feel like? What can you smell and hear and taste?

We see through our eyes more than we see with them. If you see a telescope, you know what it is, and why. Your little sister may not. Because she does not know what a telescope is, she can't draw it as well as you can, even if she is more skilled in drawing than you are. Both of you draw from your own experience with the thing you are drawing.

Watch a baby. He touches and tastes everything he sees. That is how he sees.

Try this "seeing" experiment:

Close your eyes as soon as you have read the next two sentences. Keep them closed and exchange your object with that of a partner. Return your partner's object before opening your eyes, and then draw it from memory.

Partner's Object

Name _____ Date _____

Ways of Seeing *(cont.)*

Practice looking—using your eyes to see in different ways. Close your eyes again and hold your object close to your nose. Open your eyes and very slowly move your object away from you . . . straight out.

1. Draw what you see up close.

2. Draw what you see when it is six to ten inches (15 to 25 cm) away from your face.

3. Draw what you see when it is at arm's length.

Study your three drawings and consider where you would place each on an abstraction ladder. Discuss with a partner or your group.

Name _____ Date _____

Ways of Seeing *(cont.)*

Psychics speak of seeing auras around people. Actually, everyone has an energy field surrounding him. An aura is a person's energy field which varies according to his energy level at the moment. Some say that if you want to, you can learn to see auras by relaxing and looking long enough at someone standing in front of a blank wall.

Practice seeing with other senses.

Close your eyes again and feel your object. (You do not have to taste it if you do not want to.) Concentrate on your tactile sense for a few minutes.

Now, quickly draw your object again without looking at it.

```



```

Smell your object. You may have to close your eyes again to detect a scent. If you have a cold, imagine what it smells like. According to its smell, what color would you give it? _____

Personify your object. Give it a nickname. _____

Imagine you are mad at your object. Pretend it did something wrong.

On the following lines, scold your object—write out your scathing diatribe.

_____

_____

_____

_____

_____

Name _____ Date _____

Ways of Seeing *(cont.)*

Imagine how your object responded to your diatribe. Write what it would do, say, or think.

_____

_____

_____

_____

_____

_____

Listen to its tone of voice. What does it sound like?

_____

_____

Draw what it sounds like below, and color how it feels.

Name _____ Date _____

Ways of Seeing *(cont.)*

Cartooning Expression: On each of the blank ovals, use no more than five lines to suggest facial expressions.

(**Note:** If available in the district library or video stores, check out the video or laser disc *The Mystery of Picasso* by Henri-Georges Clouzot, produced by Samuel Goldwyn Home Entertainment. It is a film showing Picasso drawing, shot through glass. You can watch Picasso's thinking as he works. His hand jumps all over the glass, giving viewers a fascinating lesson.)

Name _____ Date _____

Ways of Seeing *(cont.)*

Action Drawing: The way to learn to draw is by drawing. Making art takes more than knowing about it, although you do need to know. A chemist may understand the chemical reactions in foods placed over high heat, but not be able to make a decent soup. He might not be able to sense what makes up a delicious taste, as would a skilled chef.

Drawing takes lots of drawing—sometimes furiously, sometimes by taking great pains—but always drawing.

Use a soft lead pencil (3B or 4B) with a blunt, thick point and lots of 10" by 15" (25 cm x 38 cm) sheets of newsprint. Have a model volunteer to stand in front of the class and move around freely—stretching, practicing moves in football, baseball, or basketball, stooping to pick up something, dancing. As the model moves, you draw NOT WHAT YOU SEE BUT WHAT THE MODEL IS DOING.

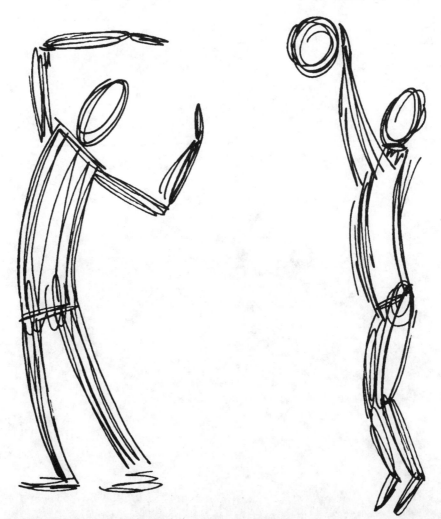

Feel how the model lifts or droops, pushes forward, pulls back, drops down. A drawing of a prize fighter would show the push, from foot to fist, behind his blows.

Name _____ Date _____

Ways of Seeing *(cont.)*

There may be nothing in your drawing to suggest the shape of the model. That does not matter. It is only the action, the gesture that you are responding to, fast and furiously. You must feel that the gesture is moving. Your drawing should have no exact shape or edges.

To see the gesture you must be able to feel it in your own body. If you don't "feel it," you can't understand what you see.

A gesture drawing is like scribbling, rather than printing. You think more about the meaning of the movement than of the way the mover looks.

It does not matter where you begin to draw because you are drawing fast, drawing the whole figure immediately. Start with the feet. Feel the upward push. In the first five seconds, draw something that indicates part of the body in the pose.

Name _____ Date _____

Copying a Masterpiece

When you want to learn how to write fiction, you should try copying a few pages of your favorite piece of fiction, including all punctuation and paragraphing. If you want to write movie scripts, you should try copying a script. Not only do you learn the format, you also pick up a sense of what is important to keep and what to discard. Then, after you have finished your copy, you release your own spontaneous self and forget what you have been copying.

To begin: On this page, draw from memory Leonardo da Vinci's *Mona Lisa*. (If you have never seen a reproduction of this famous painting, draw the arms, neck, shoulders, and head of a woman facing you.)

Name _____ Date _____

Copying a Masterpiece *(cont.)*

Now look at the reproduction of the *Mona Lisa* and draw her again. If you have coloring materials, copy the colors also.

Compare your memory to your copy. Note where her eyes are in her head. Note the position of her arms. How close were you?

Compare your drawings with those of your classmates.

Now, ask your teacher to give you individual reproductions of work by Salvador Dali or Magritte or Edward Hopper or Picasso or Renoir or Van Gogh or Gauguin or Carravagio or Michelangelo. Choose one you particularly like and spend the rest of the class time copying it.

Name _____ Date _____

Five Sorts of Drawing

1. **Observation:** After school, pick three things you see that you would like to draw. Sketch all three, either with contour or gesture drawing; then decide on the one you want to complete for your portfolio.

2. **Memory:** Recall a picture of yourself when you were little. Draw it from memory on this page. When you go home, find the actual picture and draw it again. Put both drawings in your portfolio.

Me

Art

Name _____ Date _____

Five Sorts of Drawing *(cont.)*

3. **Imagination:** Ask your teacher to play some classical music that is not too familiar; draw whatever comes to mind as you listen. Let your imagination fly.

  • Create a creature.

  • Design a building that grows according to use.

  • "Take a line for a walk," as Paul Klee said, and see where it goes and what it makes.
    Put your best imaginative drawing in your portfolio. Title it "Imaginative Drawing."

4. **Verbal to Visual:** Have a volunteer read aloud the opening two or three pages of "Laddru's Dare" in the Language section. Draw a picture of Laddru below.

When you have drawn her thoroughly and to your satisfaction, go back to the story and add the words that complete your picture of her.

Name _____ Date _____

Five Sorts of Drawing *(cont.)*

4. **Verbal to Visual** *(cont.):*

Picture the front entrance of your school. Sketch it below from memory. Next, imagine that a 20-foot (6 M) wide slide comes down from the roof of your school to the ground in front of the entrance. Sketch it in. Imagine a school band with each member of the band carrying an instrument and sliding down that twenty-foot slide. Draw in that sliding crowd of musicians. Let them overlap.

Name _____ Date _____

Five Sorts of Drawing *(cont.)*

5. **Experimental:** Just as writing can be an act of discovery, so can experimental drawing. Look at the works of art on the walls, on the television monitor, or in your books. Choose three or four to study. Consider and discuss the design, the artist's technique, the symbolism, the feeling expressed, and the meaning of each.

- What does each work suggest for the future?

- What new images come to mind?

Draw a new image below that any one of your chosen works might suggest.

Art and Scientific Method

You recall the stages of the scientific model from your science class. Now, let us try it with one of your drawings.

Choose from your portfolio a drawing you particularly like.

Step One: Observe. Look at it closely.

Step Two: Analyze. Take it apart. Measure its parts. Draw its parts on separate paper. Enlarge them . . . shrink them. How do the parts relate to the whole?

Step Three: Synthesize. Put the parts back together, perhaps in a new way.

Step Four: Test. Show your synthesized drawing to art teachers and artists wherever you can find them. Ask them to critique it, to say how and where it works and how and where it does not work as well as it could. Remember, they will be critiquing your drawing, not you.

Next, try applying this procedure to a self-portrait. Use a copy machine to enlarge a clear photo of your face.

Observe: Examine the enlargement closely.

Analyze: Copy its parts. Note where your eyes are in relation to your hairline.

Synthesize: Draw it all together; but, without changing facial expression in the enlarged photo, change the feeling behind it by actually feeling intensely good or bad as you draw the synthesized portrait.

Test: Ask your classmates to guess the emotion behind the facade of your face.

An actor, to convey the personality and mood of the character he is playing, must step out of his own mood and personality and feel the role he is playing. As you practice adopting a mood for your drawing, you will soon see that with a line or two you can convey that mood. What are the moods of the lines below?

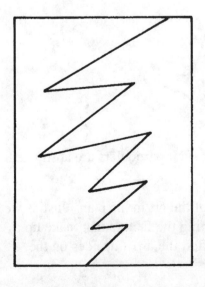 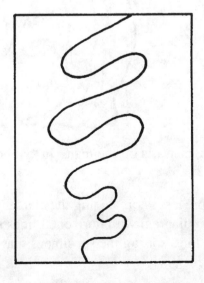 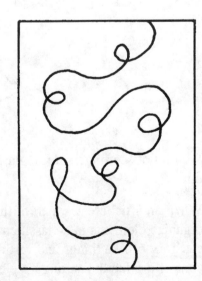

Writing About Art

Place within your reach the vocabulary of art from this chapter. Add to your understanding of the language three terms: *unity, economy,* and *aesthetic sense.* Let us consider how each term applies to art.

Unity

Unity means oneness—the sense of a whole. A human body consists of 90% water. We do not usually think of ourselves as water or as the sum of our bones, organs, and muscles. We see ourselves as single units. You could say our skin unifies us, makes us whole. Even with skin, we have dangling appendages represented by this abstract symbol for man based on a famous drawing by Leonardo da Vinci:

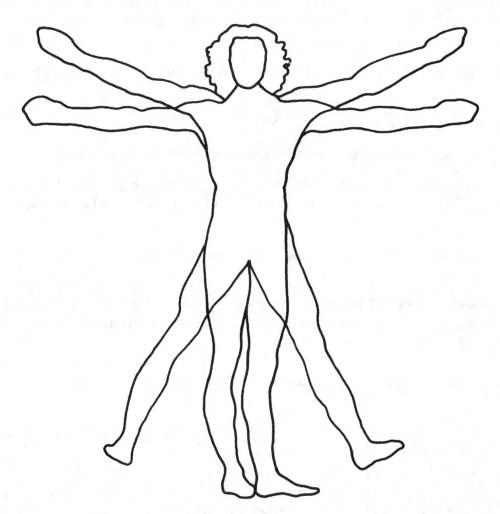

We do not see fingers, toes, glasses, or warts on the man. In symbols, such particulars are abstracted out.

When an artist creates, part of the process is organizing the elements of the art in his plan. Just as we organize elements in a classification diagram with horizontal lines sorting the factors that make up a category of like things and vertical lines sorting the specimens that differ, the artist decides on the controlling factors among his elements.

146

Writing About Art *(cont.)*

Organization consists of developing unity out of the specimens. For example, if the artist has two opposing types of lines among his elements, vertical and horizontal, he can bring them into a unified whole by using another straight line that is neither vertical nor horizontal. This works because this other straight line is of the same sort or class of line. A curved line would not provide unity because it is not of the same class as the other lines.

If you have a series of artistic elements you want to use, make a classification diagram of the elements. It will help you choose what you need for unity.

Economy

Economy echoes unity and is vital to it. You begin with a whole lot of parts that remind you of your bedroom when the clutter overwhelms you. You start tossing out what you do not need. In other words, you sort.

In painting, you eliminate all elements that do not relate to the composition as a whole.

In expository writing about how to make a peanut butter sandwich, for example, you would leave out sentences about anchovies.

Economy in art is often associated with the word *abstraction*. The artist abstracts—pulls out—particular specimens to simplify the meaning, to give meaning to the feeling.

Aesthetic Sense

When the artist succeeds, his work *resonates* for many people. Can you recall a movie whose images stayed with you for months? Years? Can you think of a movie that you forgot as soon as you walked out of the theater? Many persons have rented videos of movies only to discover they had already seen them and forgotten them.

Works of art that are eminently forgettable do not resonate. We have no desire to see, read, or hear them again. They lack aesthetic value.

Works that do resonate are meaningful to us. They seem to remain part of us after we have left them. For us, then, they have aesthetic value. We do not need to have been raised in Ancient Greece, for example, to feel the aesthetic value of the Parthenon.

One American traveler relates the following illustrative story.

In a small museum of modern art in Athens, Greece, I saw a painting of a woman who seemed to be weeping. Yet, I couldn't find a single tear on her face. Somehow the artist suggested the tears. That painting still resonates for me. I was alone when I saw it; once in a while you should be alone in an art museum to develop your aesthetic sense.

Writing About Art *(cont.)*

The positive side to visiting art museums is obvious. They are wonderful places to explore. There can be a negative side to visiting art museums, however, for they are institutions, not works of art. Consider, for example, Michael Ventura's thoughts about his boyhood in the Bronx and visits to New York City in the following passage from "Dance Among the Ruins."

My mother took me to museums often (the city museums were free in those days). I loved the Museum of Natural History, the dinosaurs especially; I thought of them as enormous rats, I fought them in my fantasies. But the Metropolitan Museum of Art—my mother loved it, but it made me afraid. The people there were different. Our best clothes weren't as good as their casuals. They spoke strangely, so clearly and carefully. No matter what their words said, their voices sounded flat and bored. And if they spoke to us, it was with that slight thickening of the voice that people have when they visit the sick in hospitals. We were treated with a deference that dismissed us.

"But it was the art that made me most afraid. What was it about? Who was it about?" Here and there I would recognize something almost human, almost natural ("natural" for me meant the street); but "almost" wasn't near enough. Every hall, every wall, had one message for me, and it was the same message I saw on television: "You don't exist."

"You can see the contradiction in the sentence. In order to say, "You don't exist," there has to be a "you" to say it to. So you do exist: you exist just enough to be told that you don't. They will entice you into the museum, but within the museum they will obliterate you; they will seduce you with television, but on television you will either be denied or lied about. The shrinks tell us that the surest way to drive people crazy is to give them a double signal: two contradictory messages at the same time. The poor know that this theory is correct.

"Even to a boy it was clear that the museum thought itself superior to the television, but both institutions wanted nothing to do with my people, the working people of the street, without whom the world does not function; so the museum seemed to me a quieter, more spacious, more dignified version of the television. Television bombards us with negative images of anyone excluded from affluence, while the museum defines "beauty" as anything accepted by affluence. To be led by the hand into what is advertised as the palace of beauty, and to see no image of one's kind or one's world, is to be told in no uncertain terms that you are not beautiful.

"You're supposed to appreciate this. You're supposed to take this in as knowledge, and be grateful for it. And you try, because God knows you're hungry for beauty, and the way the painting is being used is not the painting's fault. But the institution changes the power and the inflection of its beauty."

148

Writing About Art *(cont.)*

Following are three writing prompts. Read them all, choose one, and write your heart out. After the third prompt on page 150, you will find directions for concluding art activities centered around logos, masks, and portfolios.

Prompt A: Select a painting or drawing you particularly like, either your own or one of the masters. Using many of the words in your Vocabulary of Art, write an essay describing the work.

Process: Choose the work and talk about it in detail in your group or with a partner. Write your first draft. Have a classmate score it according to the rubric and then rewrite.

Scoring Rubric for Prompt A

1. The writer describes the work completely so that the reader can picture it.

2. The writer includes discussion of the major elements of the work and how they are organized to achieve unity.

3. The writer includes the general meaning of the work and how it translates feeling into meaning.

4. The writer follows standard conventions for written communication. (complete sentences, clear spelling, relationship between general and specific statements.)

(All four points = A, three = B, two = C, and one = D)

Prompt B: Using Michael Ventura's writing as a model, describe an experience you had at an art museum or with a particular work of art.

Process: Talk about the experience to your partner. Write your first draft. Have a classmate score it according to the rubric and rewrite.

Scoring Rubric for Prompt B

1. The writer opens with a clear description of time and place.

2. The writer includes enough details to support a point of view.

3. The writer includes terms from the vocabulary of art.

4. The writer follows conventions of written expression.

Writing About Art (cont.)

Prompt C: Write an essay on the relationship of a particular school of art to the technology of the period—for example, Renaissance, impressionism, cubism, abstract expression. Illustrate your thesis with descriptions of one or two famous works.

Process: Re-read the section on art history. Read other available sources. Interview people interested in the subject and write a first draft.

Scoring Rubric for Prompt C

1. The writer opens with a general discussion: how art reflects the technology of the chosen period of time.

2. The writer supports his thesis with specific descriptions of the given technology and its general effect.

3. The writer supports his thesis with descriptions of specific works of art and uses terms from the vocabulary of art.

4. The writer follows conventions of written communication.

Because of the relative difficulty of Prompt C, you deserve extra credit or a generous grading policy for trying it.

Concluding Activities—Art

Symbols and Logos

A. Start collecting logos. You will find them in magazine advertisements. What is McDonald's logo? Does it relate in anyway to a hamburger? It does resemble an M. What else does it symbolize?

B. When you have a collection of ten logos, start creating your own for the mythology you are writing for your school. Put your best one in your portfolio. Start a school-wide contest for the most appropriate logo.

Final Mask

Draw another Halloween mask on a separate sheet of paper. After you have compared the two, attach it to your original and put it in your portfolio.

Portfolio Exchange

Exchange portfolios with a partner—several partners if you have time—and pay a compliment or two.

The Language and Beauty of Mathematics

Imagine a class full of students clamoring to learn more math, chanting, "Teach us, show us, teach us, show us. We want homework! Give us homework!"

When your students were in first grade, they wanted to learn everything. Many of them, somewhere along the line, decided they could not learn mathematics. Other disciplines, yes. Math, no. "I just don't have a head for figures," they say.

It is part of the mythology of intelligence. We have heard about learning styles, cognitive development, Piaget, meta-cognition, multiple intelligences, left brain/right brain functions—all the scholarly explanations, ad infinitum. Study upon study. All are interesting and valid within context. But, if a student decides he cannot do math, he joins the ranks of innumerates whose number is legion. There are billions of us.

Can educators change a student's self-concept? Deeper than attitude, self-concept will not respond to a pep talk, the lure of good grades, or the fear of bad grades. Deficiency in any one endeavor—and it is quite often math—becomes part of the student's identity. When this happens, it limits him or her for life. How can educators prevent that identity formation?

According to a consensus of mathematics educators, students will respond to a four-pronged approach to teaching mathematics—if the approach starts in the early grades and continues year after year. (Willoughby, *Mathematics Education for a Changing World*)

The four steps students should be allowed to take to truly learn math and be willing to use it in daily problem-solving follow:

1. Derive the mathematics from the student's own reality.

2. Discover and use the power of abstract thought.

3. Practice, practice, practice.

4. Apply mathematics to something of student interest.

Step One: To accomplish this, you have to discover just what your students' realities are—not a simple task. One approach is to use a short pretest appropriate to grade level and demand that each student write his thoughts and the steps he took to solve each problem. This will give you an indication of your students' realities. For example, here is one item on such a test:

If a gallon of paint covers 250 square feet (22.5 sq. M), how much paint would you have to buy to paint four walls that are 8 feet (2.4 M) high, 12 feet (3.6 M) wide, and 14 feet (4.19 M) long?

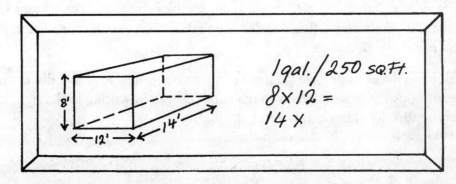

The Language and Beauty of Mathematics *(cont.)*

One student might write, "First, I have to multiply 8 by 12 by 14 to get the number of feet to paint. But would that be square feet? What's square feet? But then I'd get a sum for only half of the wall space. But I don't know whether to divide that sum times two into 250 or 250 into the sum."

Another student might write, "I would multiply 8 x 12 to get the square feet on the short wall—96, and 8 x 14 to get the square footage of the long wall—112, and then add those to get 208. Double that for all four walls and you get 416. Then I'd divide 216 by 250 to decide how many gallons to buy. Since that number is 1.664, I would have to buy more than one and one-half gallons to finish the job."

After you have read your students' pretests, you will know what kind of teaching you must do and what kind of practice they need. Also, you might tell your students that mathematics is a lazy way to solve problems and ask them to give you examples that support that idea.

Step Two—Abstraction. The power and beauty of mathematics come from its level of abstraction. Suppose we used different kinds of numbers for counting dogs, for cats, for people, and for couches. We would discover that two dogs in one room and three in another in the same house add up to five dogs in the house. Two cats in one room and three in another would add up to five cats, but we would not be able to generalize, or abstract, the fact that two plus three equals five. The fact that numbers are independent of the things they are counting means they are abstracted out of the pile of things. This gives numbers their power. They can travel anywhere. And they are much lighter than couches or anything else they stand for.

As in language, composition, art, science, and social studies, students need to scamper up and down the abstraction ladder so they do not lose sight of either end. They need to become aware that manipulatives are concrete and valuable, just as numbers are abstract and valuable.

Step Three: This is a given. Students need time specified for regular practice.

Step Four: Use realistic applications. Ask students to describe their routes to school and explain why they chose them over other possible routes. Ask them to guess probabilities by working with partners—flipping a coin and recording how often it comes up heads in a five minute span. Ask students to volunteer current problems they would like to solve and have them estimate the level of abstraction involved.

Portfolio Assessment

Portfolio assessment of collaborative problem-solving finesses cheating. The lessons suggest how. When tests are student-administered to assess learning rather than to determine letter grades, attitudes improve, and there is no need to cheat.

You may read aloud to the class or have student collaborative groups read and discuss the text. The single column text following is for students to read and react to in writing in the right hand column. Student pages are headed by Name and Date.

Name _____ Date _____

Counting on Fingers

Read the following and write comments, figures, or equations in the right-hand column.

Explanation

In the beginning was the number one: *un, une, uno, unity*. With that we began counting and discovered there is also less than one: *zero*.

Watch a toddler count. If you ask how old he is, he will hold up two, three, or four fingers. By the time he is five, he will say the word *five*. Our fingers are great counters. Children who use them in the early grades for simple operations can spend their time and thought on more advanced ideas later on. Children who are told in first grade to avoid their fingers when adding or subtracting will decide that using fingers is a subversive activity. Naturally, they will continue to use their fingers, but secretly. So let us use them openly.

In *Mathematics Education for a Changing World*, Professor Willoughby writes, *"An efficient way to teach young children to add involves always using the same fingers to stand for given numbers. Thus, the thumb up on the right hand is always used to represent one. The thumb and forefinger on the right hand always represent two. The thumb, forefinger, and middle finger represent three.*

All the fingers on the right hand except the little finger are used to represent four, and all the fingers on the right hand are used to represent five. Continuing in the same way, the fingers on the right hand combined with the thumb of the left hand represent six, the fingers on the right hand plus the thumb and forefinger of the left hand represent seven, and so on.

Once we have learned these "fingers sets," if we want to know what 6 + 3 is, we can start by putting up the finger set for six without the need to count. Then we can count on as we put up more fingers: "one (left forefinger goes up), two (left middle finger goes up), three (left ring finger goes up.)" Now, we know without counting that we have the finger set for nine, so we know that 6 + 3 = 9. (page 20)

Comments/Questions/Sketches

Counting on Fingers *(cont.)*

Each of your fingers has three segments. If you count each segment on each hand, you can count to 30. It is easy to count to 30 on your fingers, but a bit more complex to count to 255. Let's look at how.

Everything in nature, including computers, uses the binary system: 0 or 1, off and on. Use the binary system and your bendable fingers as follows:

Binary System (first column)

0 = finger down 1 = finger up

Decimal System (second column)

Right Hand	Binary	Decimal	Decimal Powers
All fingers down	0	0	0
1st, or forefinger, up	1	1	2^0
2nd up	10	2	2^1
1st & 2nd up	11	3	
3rd up	100	4	2^2
1st & 3rd up	101	5	
2nd & 3rd up	110	6	
1st, 2nd & 3rd up	111	7	
4th up	1000	8	2^3
4th & 1st	1001	9	
4th & 2nd	1010	10	
4th, 2nd & 1st	1011	11	
4th & 3rd	1100	12	
4th, 3rd & 1st	1101	13	
4th, 3rd & 2nd	1110	14	
4th, 3rd, 2nd & 1st	1111	15	

Left Hand (skipping some of the above steps—which ones?)			
5th or forefinger up	10,000	16	2^4
6th up	100,000	32	2^5
7th up	1,000,000	64	2^6
8th up	10,000,000	128	2^7

The sum of all eight fingers equals 256.

154

Name _____ Date _____

Counting on Fingers *(cont.)*

In your group and in the space below, go through the procedure outlined on the previous page and draw the fingers for each hand. Practice with each other until you can easily count on your fingers. Ask for help, whether or not you need it. When you are sure you understand it, put this page in your portfolio.

Name _____ Date _____

Growth and Numeracy

In the Beginning

The first thing you ever did way back when you were a cell was add food and subtract waste. Then after you added and subtracted, you grew, divided, and multiplied.

So, you see that our wills, our desires, our very ideas of ourselves have no effect, for we are mathemetical beings whether we like it or not.

We can choose to be innumerates—to be so ignorant of how numbers work that we cannot read them. Though I am not illiterate, I realized when reading John Allen Paulo's book *Innumeracy* that I am innumerate. When I read newspaper accounts that include extremely large numbers, I do not understand the significance of the information. And without an educated understanding of probabilities I might think driving a car is safer than going to war. It is not.

In *Innumeracy*, Paulos discusses the possibility of extraterrestrial life. He writes, *If intelligence developed naturally on Earth, it is difficult to see why the same process wouldn't have occurred elsewhere. What's needed is a system of physical elements capable of many different combinations, and a source of energy through the system.*

The energy flux causes the system to "explore" various combinations of possibilities, until a small collection of stable, complex, energy-storing molecules develops, followed by the chemical evolution of more complex compounds, including some amino acids, from which proteins are constructed. Eventually, primitive life develops, and then shopping malls. (page 59)

It may seem like quite a leap from primitive cell development to shopping malls, but is it? Growth is not an orderly, linear process. Growth is proliferation—random, out of control. Are your feet growing faster than your brain? Nothing you can do about it. But you can determine the ratio of the size of your feet to the size of your brain—that is, if you want to.

Comments, Questions

_____

_____

_____

_____

_____

_____

_____

_____

_____

_____

_____

_____

_____

_____

_____

_____

_____

_____

_____

_____

_____

156

Name _____ Date _____

Growth and Numeracy *(cont.)*

In the Beginning

Paulos writes, *The size of a human cell is to that of a person as a person's size is to that of Rhode Island. Likewise, a virus is to a person as a person is to the Earth.*

In the form we use to analyze metaphors:

$$\frac{\text{cell}}{\text{person}} :: \frac{\text{person's size}}{\text{Rhode Island}}$$

$$\frac{\text{virus}}{\text{person}} :: \frac{\text{person}}{\text{Earth}}$$

And an atom is to a person as a person is to the Earth's orbit around the sun; a proton is to a person as a person is to the distance from Earth to Alpha Centauri, the nearest star outside our solar system. (page 16)

When we are numerate, we can imagine what huge numbers mean. Paulos writes, "*. . . knowing that it takes only about eleven and a half days for a million seconds to tick away, whereas almost thirty-two years are required for a billion seconds to pass, gives one a better grasp of the relative magnitudes of these two common numbers. What about trillions?*" (page 11)

Comments, Questions

_____

_____

_____

_____

_____

_____

_____

_____

_____

_____

_____

_____

_____

_____

_____

_____

◆ ◆ ◆ ◆

Fill in the blanks below to show the relative sizes of things—such as, an ant is to an oak tree as a puppy is to an elephant. Make up your own first; then, share in your group.

_____ :: _____

_____ :: _____

_____ :: _____

Name _____ Date _____

Venus and Earth

The *Magellan* space probe gave us incredible amounts of information about Venus. Venus is Earth's closest planetary neighbor. It formed at about the same time as Earth and from the same gaseous nebula. Both planets have been shaped by volcanism and the bombardment of meteors.

Characteristic	Venus	Earth
Atmosphere	carbon dioxide, nitrogen	oxygen, nitrogen
Air pressure	1,288 pounds per square inch	14 pounds per square inch at sea level
Distance from sun	67.1 million miles (107.4 million km)	93.2 million miles (149 million km)
Rotation period	243 Earth days	24 hours
Rotation type	east to west	west to east
Surface temperature	890°F (476°C)	80°F (27°C)

On the lines below, create a character for your sci-fi story who could live on Venus. What kind of problems would your character have? Be sure to take into consideration all the facts in the above table.

_____

_____

_____

_____

_____

_____

_____

_____

_____

_____

Discuss your creation with members of your group. Add to your character description, use it in other classes, and place it in your portfolio for math.

Leverage

Recall from your English classes that a definition has two parts. One is fixed and is usually the first sense given in a dictionary. The other changes and depends on outside conditions or context.

The word *leverage* comes from *lever* which, as a verb, means "to raise or pry up." As a noun, it is a thing, a tool, a pry bar. In science, a lever is a tool, a rigid piece that transmits and modifies force when forces are applied at two points and it turns on a third (the *fulcrum*). Leverage is the mechanical advantage gained by a lever.

Remember when you were little and liked to play on a seesaw? Remember what happened when a bigger kid who weighed a lot more than you got on the other side? Leverage changed.

Scientists determine the "work" of leverage by multiplying the weight or force in one direction times the distance from the fulcrum. The longer the distance, the greater the leverage. Or, when force is applied far from the fulcrum, the advantage is multiplied.

Stand now for a minute and hold a hardcover book close to your chest. Next hold the book with your arms outstretched. Although the book weighs the same, it feels heavier when your arms are outstretched.

Expanding the concept: Historians often say that Ancient Greece is the cradle of Western Civilization. Archimedes, the Einstein of Ancient Greece, said, "Give me a lever long enough, and I can move the world." If you consider that Archimedes' brain power acted on the world and forced people to think, you could say his brain was a "lever."

Have you ever known a secret about a brother or sister and threatened to tell your mother or father if the brother or sister would not do or give you something you wanted? That secret gave you leverage—a little more power.

If politicians have a great number of people they can count on to vote for them every election, they have "political leverage." How does the word *leverage* change from the physical universe to the political? It begins in the physical, and through analogy it works in other contexts.

In your group, brainstorm other uses of the word *leverage,* other contexts where it is used to express force or power or advantage. How does understanding how numbers work give you leverage? On the next page, with the help of your group members, write 10 sentences, each with a different use of the word.

Remember the quotation from William James in the science and art chapters? "Man's chief difference from the brutes lies in the exuberant excess of his subjective propensities . . . . Prune down his extravagances, sober him, and you undo him."

Name _____ Date _____

Leverage *(cont.)*

One of man's subjective propensities is trying to control the randomness of the universe and the randomness of growth. Such control requires that we understand the disciplines of science and mathematics. Let us begin with the fundamental properties of numbers described by Archimedes: Any number can be increased by adding together enough smaller numbers, no matter how small they are.

Since Archimedes understood the property of numbers, you can see why he claimed that if he had a long enough lever and some place in the universe to stand, he could lift the Earth. The property of numbers led him to that statement, as well as the concept of leverage.

Leverage Sentences

_____

_____

_____

_____

_____

_____

_____

_____

Concept-Forming Game

Write the following problem on the board:

A respected, world-renowned scientist reports that ice cream production is doing irreparable harm to the universe, harm that will ultimately cause extinction of the human race.

Which of the people described on your cards would you put on a committee to address and possibly solve this problem? And why did you choose them? Or, why didn't you choose them? Answer on the page provided, discuss in your group, and make changes as a result of your discussion.

Reproduce the following eight statements in sufficient number for each group of students in the class, attach them to cards and laminate for use in future classes. Each group of students will rank their choices and then present a general statement explaining their selections and rejections.

Cards

Allyson says bad things happen to people in threes—three times in a row—and likes to give several examples.	Joe's mother claims she has extra-sensory perception. She makes her living as a psychic. Secretly, Joe thinks his mother makes correct guesses about her clients based on statistical probabilities.
Heather argues that people laughing and talking on the beach are not necessarily happier and more successful than she. "When we see happy people," she says, "it doesn't mean they're happy all the time. Maybe we don't see them when they're sad."	Duke likes to throw dice. He has graphed the number of times even numbers come up. He says there is a higher probability for the occurrence of coincidences in life than for even numbers to come up. For instance, he predicts that if you put 23 randomly selected people in the same room, at least two will have the same birthday.
Arnie went to a numerologist who told him he chose the day he was born as well as his own first name. Arnie liked that idea because five (the number of letters in Arnie's name) means he wants to lead a creative life. Since he saw the numerologist, Arnie has been leading a creative life.	Phyllis uses statistics to back up her beliefs. For instance, she claims that 93% of earthquakes occur when the weather is extremely calm and the barometer reads close to 76 centimeters (or 30 inches).
Roger says the price of ice cream has gone up six percent throughout the world. Therefore, the probability of global harm will decrease by six percent.	Maria can make simple calculations of large numbers in her head. Through practice she has also learned to make fairly accurate numerical estimations and to interpret the numbers on statistical probability tables.

Name _____ Date _____

Concept-Forming Game *(cont.)*

Answer below and then discuss in your group. Make changes and additions to your answers as a result of your discussion.

1. Which of the people described on your cards would you put on a committee to address and possibly solve this problem?

_____

_____

_____

_____

_____

_____

2. Why did you choose each one?

_____

_____

_____

_____

_____

_____

3. Why didn't you choose each of the others?

_____

_____

_____

_____

_____

_____

162

Abstraction and Mathematics

Let us return to the abstraction ladder: You place the most concrete things that you can see, smell, taste, feel, and hear on the lowest rung. As you categorize and create order of the chaos of sense details, you climb the ladder. (Remember, placement on any rung of the ladder is relative to the material you are sorting by generality or specificity. Don't try for an exact answer.) Where do mathematical symbols fall on the ladder? The same place language symbols fall—high up there.

In the language of mathematics, *problem solving* is at the top of the ladder, *estimating* not far below, and *general use of a calculator* below estimating. Would such specific functions as addition, multiplication, and division fall on the lowest rungs? Where do you think geometry would fall?

Geometric figures are like much of Picasso's art, recognizable as representative of something we have seen on Earth, but obviously not photographic representation.

What about calculus? Have you seen the beauty in problems solved with calculus? Some of those equations could be framed and hung on a wall as decoration. The "fundamental theorem of calculus" is used to compute the area of shapes having curved surfaces. Note the figure and equation shown below. Take out your crayons or pens and color this one:

The Fundamental Theorem of Calculus

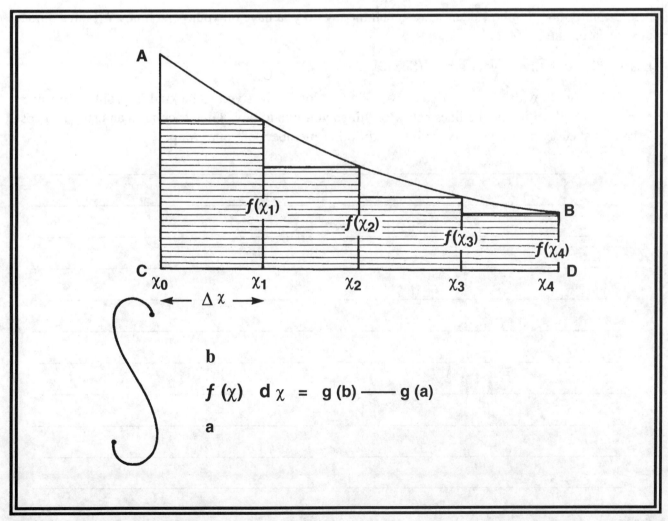

$$\int_a^b f(\chi) \, d\chi = g(b) - g(a)$$

Name _____ Date _____

Abstraction, Math, and Money

All conscious experience—whatever happens that we are aware of—is made up of *sensation* (what we discover through our senses), *emotion* (physical, visceral responses), and the *recognition of similarity* (how things are alike) *and difference,* which in humans becomes the *power of abstraction.* (How is art like an oak tree?)

Language and numbers are abstract systems of symbols, invented by humans to stand for concrete things. It is much easier to measure the size of a room and the furniture in it, use those numbers to cut out little abstracts representing the pieces of furniture, and move them around a representation of the room, than it is to actually move the furniture. It is even easier to rearrange furniture using a computer program. You don't need scissors.

It is much easier to buy a wagon with money than it is to buy it with a herd of cows.

Money is an abstraction. In and of itself, it is not worth much, is it? Yet it has been called the root of all evil, the source of all human power, the goddess, the king. Money comes in numbers. The national debt in the United States is approaching a trillion dollars—that is a debt of 1,000,000,000,000 or 10^{12} dollars.

That is pretty high up the ladder. How much money do you have on your person now? Is that amount any lower on the ladder?

Discuss that question in your group. (See teacher's key.)

What will you do with the money you have today? Money gives you some kind of problem to solve every day. Make a list on the lines below of things you like to buy. Give each item an estimated cost. When finished, compare your list with those of other members of your group.

_____   _____

_____   _____

_____   _____

_____   _____

_____   _____

_____   _____

_____   _____

_____   _____

_____   _____

_____   _____

Name _____ Date _____

Abstraction, Math, and Money *(cont.)*

Now make a list of ways you *do* get money to buy things and the ways you *could* get money.

Do	**Could**
_____	_____
_____	_____
_____	_____
_____	_____

Add to this list by comparing with those of your classmates.

Think of a few word problems typical of math tests—e.g., If a train is traveling 50 miles per hour, how long does it take to cover 25 miles?

In your group, make up several word problems for younger students that might be actual problems in their daily lives. Use your lists of money. Using numbers, generate more lists of problems in your daily experience. Think of card games where counting matters. Think of boat-building, cooking, scaling walls, sewing, replacing broken wheels, and hanging basketball nets. Have a good time and come up with some interesting problems for younger students to solve. Decide on the best from your group and create a test you can actually use.

Ask a teacher of lower grade students to administer your test. Your problems should allow for several approaches to the solutions. In math, as in life, there is usually more than one way to accomplish something.

Remember, your test questions must be valid and must involve real life experience and needs. It helps, too, if they are interesting or funny.

Let the test takers know you will be scoring their tests with a scoring guide or rubric that you design. Here is an example:

Scoring Rubric

1. The student responded to all aspects of the problem.

2. The student chose more than one approach to solve it.

3. The student took time to solve the problem.

4. The student solved part of the problem.

If the student exhibits all four points, he gets an A; three, a B; two, a C; and one, a D.

Place the best problem you write and the best student responses in your portfolio.

Music, Maestro!

On every piece of music, there is a time signature: 2/4, 3/4, 4/4, 6/8, with variations. The rhythm of beats is based on a count. Notes are based on fractions. In 4/4 time there are four beats to a measure, and each quarter note gets one beat. A half note gets two beats, and a whole note gets four. In 6/8 time there are six beats to a measure, and each eighth note gets one beat.

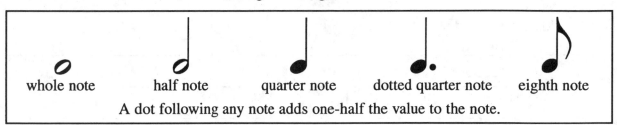

A dot following any note adds one-half the value to the note.

Mozart once wrote a waltz in which he specified 11 different possibilities for 14 of the 16 bars of the waltz and two possibilities for one of the other bars. Thus, there are 2×11^{14} variations on the waltz, only a fraction of which have ever been heard. (*Innumeracy*, page 18)

Examine the musical measures shown below. Do the notes always conform to the time signature shown at the beginning?

Can you tell what the time signature is in the second set of measures shown below?

If you play a musical instrument and are learning how to read music, bring your instruments to class and demonstrate to your group how you use math to play and math to listen and math to dance.

Numbers, Words, and Meaning

We are back to language again—semantics, the study of meaning.

Computer program designers speak of time in nanoseconds. We could, too. Geologists speak of time in billions of years. It takes some getting accustomed to the fact that the minuscule times and distances of microphysics, along with the vastness of astronomical measurements, share the dimensions of our human world.

What is the size of your bedroom? Your house? Your school? Your town, county, state, or country? Your world? Stretch your measuring tools through numbers such as 10^{-100} to 10^{100} and you will have the power to encompass your world. (In case you wanted to know, 10^{100} is called a *googol*.)

Not only does numeracy, like literacy, give you power and leverage, but it also keeps you from making costly mistakes. Ordering fertilizer for your lawn by the cubic yard would be a costly (and smelly!) mistake.

Here are some interesting facts from *Reading the Numbers* (pages 141–142) by Mary Blocksma:

Before 1958, the year when the International Committee on Weights and Measures gave us even larger measures, a mega-something was the biggest something anyone could think of. And why not? Mega is a prefix meaning million. Millionaires made megabucks, megahertz measured radio waves, and a megaphone impressively amplified sound.

Unfortunately, mega cannot begin to be used to measure our galaxy, much less the universe, so now we have giga and tera as well:

> **kilo**—*thousand (1,000)*
> **mega**—*million (1,000,000)*
> **giga**—*billion (1,000,000,000)*
> **tera**—*trillion (1,000,000,000,000)*

All these prefixes, although they sound terribly scientific, are rather charmingly based on Greek synonyms for "really large": kilo comes from the Greek word for "thousand," mega from "great," giga from "giant," and tera from "monster." Although the prefixes are commonly used with metric measures, making teragrams and gigameters and such, it is quite acceptable to attach them to nonmetric measures, making kilowatt-hours and megatons. There is an exception: Metric prefixes have a slightly different meaning in the world of computers. It shouldn't be long before these handily descriptive prefixes become common usage for "more than the mind can comprehend," with billionaires making "gigabucks," rock stars using "gigaphones," and "teradollars" describing the national debt.

Numbers, Words, and Meaning (cont.)

However far scientists have reached into the universe, they have reached even farther into the minuscule; and particle physicists require even more prefixes than astronomers. Hardly anything is more difficult to comprehend than the unseeable structure of the visible world. Still, you're probably not bothered by the things "microscopic," since you can see them through a microscope. Micro (meaning millionth) has come to mean "incredibly small, about as small as you can get," with spies hiding messages on microdots and libraries reducing vast card catalogs to books of microfilm.

But micro in today's known invisible world is an unwieldy prefix. Here are some others:

milli—*thousandth (0.001)*

micro—*millionth (0.000001)*

nano—*billionth (0.000000001)*

pico—*trillionth (0.000000000001)*

femto—*quardrillionth (0.000000000000001)*

atto—*quintillionth (0.000000000000000001)*

(To keep from confusing these with prefixes meaning "huge," remember that prefixes for the smallest numbers end with -o, while, except for kilo, those for the largest numbers end with -a.)

Name _____ Date _____

Reading and Writing About Mathematics

(Use the right hand column to write thoughts or questions about the reading.)

Game Theory

The 1994 Nobel Prize in Economics was awarded to three economists for their work on game theory which explores human behavior ranging from a poker game to a telecommuted meeting of corporate leaders in the global marketplace. The winners—John C. Harsanyi, John F. Nash, and Reinhard Selten—are experts in game theory which applies complex logic to real-world scenarios of conflict and competition. These include military strategy, politics, and sports as well as a variety and broad range of business problems.

The idea is to apply logic to the process of understanding the strategies of your opponent or rival. If you do understand his strategies, you have a better than even chance of predicting the outcome and potential benefits of a given "game."

Based on actual strategies for card games, game theory assumes that people attempt to gamble, bluff their opponents, and second guess them. Computers create complex scenarios that are abstract enough to apply to all such strategy-loaded interactions and print them in the language of mathematics.

Military analysts in World War II used game theory to predict where U.S. ships could safely cross the Atlantic. Game theory later became a major part of Cold War thinking, of U.S. nuclear strategy against the Soviets.

Since the 1970's, corporations have increasingly used game theory to decide on pricing, bidding, and other strategies.

Airlines use it during price wars to calculate their rivals' plans and determine which course of action will prove most profitable.

Companies use it when considering a new product. They believe it gives them an advantage over their competition.

Thoughts and Questions

_____

_____

_____

_____

_____

_____

_____

_____

_____

_____

_____

_____

_____

_____

_____

_____

_____

_____

_____

_____

_____

_____

Reading and Writing About Mathematics *(cont.)*

Game Theory *(cont.)*

Game theory is changing the way many people think about the economy. We used to think about economics as supply and demand only, and scarcity. To understand economics, we would picture one person on an island, figuring out what to do about scarcity.

In contrast, game theory is about lots of people dependent on one another and coping with others' strategies.

For example, if you hide a coin in your hand and ask a friend to guess which hand, you are trying to outsmart your friend. That is game theory. If you are playing football, you try to guess your opponent's next play so you can plan a way to ruin it. That is game theory, too.

Using mathematics, game theory becomes a remarkably precise tool to help us predict how our opponents will react under the rules of the game.

Thoughts and Questions

_____

_____

_____

_____

_____

_____

_____

_____

_____

_____

_____

◆ ◆ ◆ ◆

Writing

Using the above story and your own experience in the world, write a paragraph or two in which you attempt to persuade your teacher to provide regular class time for chess and card games.

Discuss the writing prompt in your group for 10 minutes; then separate to begin writing. Check your first draft against the following rubric; then rewrite and submit for your portfolio.

Scoring Rubric

1. The writer opens with a complex sentence that contains the germ of his argument.

2. The writer supports his argument with concrete details from his own experience.

3. The writer supports his argument with quotations from the article on game theory.

4. The writer follows conventions of written expression.

Extra credit: The writer includes observations of gender bias in game theory.

End of Chapter Test

1. Imagine you have a business on campus selling milk shakes at class breaks. Your competitor across the street from the campus has two employees who work with him for two hours a day. It takes each of them five minutes to make a milk shake. He claims he sold 6,000 milk shakes in three months. Assuming enough people come by, is this a reasonable claim?

   Figure it out on scrap paper, decide on your answer, and be prepared to explain your answer to the class.

2. (From Willoughby, page 101)

   Preliminary information:

   A. I have 10 fingers altogether and, for this test, assume everybody else does. That is, I do count thumbs as fingers, so I have a total of exactly 10 fingers, not eight.

   B. Chris (a second grade teacher) and Pat (a mathematician) are married and have a four-year-old daughter, Wendy. One day Chris came home and found Pat teaching Wendy the addition factors, whereupon Chris said: "You really shouldn't do that until we are sure she conserves number—you may be doing more harm than good."

Questions

1. Write a four-letter word beginning with "J" for an amusing anecdote.

   _____

2. Write a four-letter word starting with "Y" that is sometimes used to refer to a pair of oxen and is sometimes applied to a wooden frame holding the two oxen together. (Spelling counts.)

   _____

3. What do we call the white of an egg? (Spelling counts.)

   _____

   _____

4. How many fingers are there on ten hands?

   _____

5. What is Wendy's mother's name? (Do not look back at the story.)

   _____

   _____

6. What do we call the yellow of an egg? (Do not change any previous answers.)

   _____

   _____

Growth and the Constancy of Change

The following lessons are designed to elicit struggling and deepening reasoning instead of "right" answers. They are designed, also, for group problem solving and portfolio evaluation. Where appropriate, suggested answers are included in the key.

In social studies, use of the abstraction ladder is crucial to understand the political and cultural barriers that divide people and cause conflict, even though students may find it difficult until they use it often enough to fully comprehend the metaphor. It is crucial in learning how to discern the common qualities that unite us.

The lessons here are intended to illustrate the connections between ideas and behavior—the behavior of individuals and of whole nations, the consequences of some of the most insignificant choices, and the consequences of conflicting belief systems.

The first lesson asks for a history of each student's "wars," a history of conflict that may later be compared (abstracted) with the history of a country's conflict. Since students may choose which of their conflicts they wish to record or may invent some if the question seems intrusive, the consequences of the activity are benign.

The abstract concept of power and the constancy of change in the study of the world's people should be related to the self-study of a work group. Group process skills are political skills that students need to learn. Their efforts in developing these skills should be rewarded. In social studies, there is no right or wrong answer, only growth and change and portfolio assessment of each student's growth in climbing the abstraction ladder.

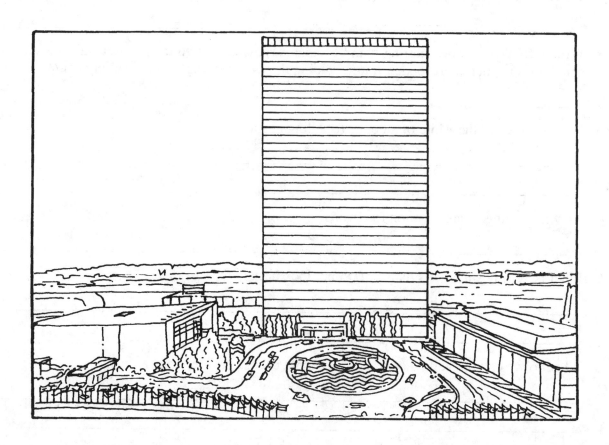

Name _____ Date _____

Conflict

Talk about a messy abstraction ladder! At least we know what math is in all its abstract beauty. But social studies is what—history? geography? politics? psychology? economics? sociology? anthropology? archeology?

The answer is all of the above; they are all connected.

Social studies is an awesome collection of stories about people working, fighting, cooperating, growing, changing, inventing, tolerating, and struggling for centuries. And at the heart of these stories is conflict.

As you proceed through this section, consider this question: *Are social systems progressing or simply recycling?*

◆ ◆ ◆ ◆

First, on the lines below, write your personal history, the story of your conflicts. List the major battles you have fought (they need not be physical), their causes, their outcomes, and their consequences. Make them up if you want to. Just make them credible. Then write about the wars you successfully avoided.

My Wars

_____

_____

_____

_____

_____

_____

Wars I Successfully Avoided

_____

_____

_____

_____

_____

_____

Name _____ Date _____

Conflict *(cont.)*

Now with the help of the other members of your group, write the history of your own country's major wars. List each war, its causes, outcomes, and consequences.

My Country's Wars

_____

_____

_____

_____

_____

_____

Wars My Country Avoided

_____

_____

_____

_____

_____

_____

_____

How is the history of your wars like the history of your country's wars? What do they have in common?

_____

_____

_____

_____

_____

_____

Name _____ Date _____

Power

According to the *Oxford English Dictionary*, the current spelling of *power* began in 1325. The word comes from the Latin *Potere* which in the 8th Century supplanted *posse,* meaning "to be able."

Following is a series of definitions from the current *American Heritage Dictionary.*

Power (noun)

1. The ability or capacity to act or perform effectively.

2. A specific capacity, faculty, or aptitude: his powers of concentration.

3. Strength or force exerted; might.

4. The ability or official capacity to exercise control; authority.

5. A person, group, or nation having great influence or control over others.

6. The might of a nation, political organization, or similar group.

7. Forcefulness; effectiveness.

8. Physics. The rate at which work is done, mathematically expressed as the first derivative of work with aspect to time and commonly measured in units such as the watt and horsepower.

9. Electricity. a. The product of applied potential difference and current in a direct-current circuit. b. The product of the effective values of the voltage and current with the cosine of the phase angle between current and voltage in alternating-current circuit.

10. Mathematics. a. An exponent. b. The number of elements in a finite set.

11. Optics. A measure of the magnification of an optical instrument, as a microscope or telescope.

12. Theology. The sixth group of angels in the hierarchical order of nine.

As you can see, the word has several levels of abstraction. On the abstraction ladder to the right, place the number of each definition on the appropriate rung, from the most abstract at the top to the most concrete at the bottom.

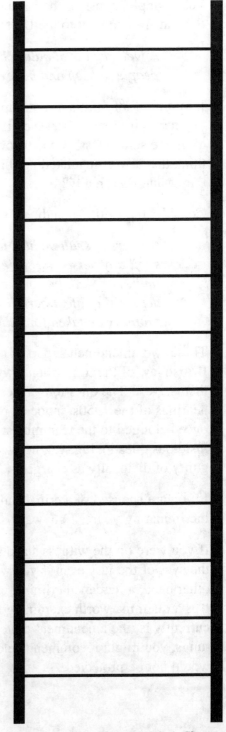

Truth Detectors

The greatest skill we learn in school or anywhere is how to pierce the fabric of falsehoods to get at the truth—how to get beyond political slogans, sound bites, and bumper sticker mentality.

The metaphor of the abstraction ladder helps us see varying levels of generality and specificity. The metaphor of classification helps us see which concepts are in the same class. When we hear or read bumper sticker thoughts, we can consider the class definition and the degree of specificity inherent in them and "see" through them.

For example, consider the issue of gun control and the slogans on both sides of it. Then read the Second Amendment to the U.S. Constitution:

> *A well-regulated militia being necessary to the security of a free state, the right of the people to keep and bear arms shall not be infringed.*

If you think of militia as a group of local citizens with guns, you might think that outlawing guns would be unconstitutional. However, if you look at the word historically, you might see that militia is not at all in the same class as people owning guns to protect private property. Bumper stickers would have us think that a well-regulated militia is in the same class as Americans being able to buy whatever guns they want. Is it really?

Consider the Fifth Amendment to the U.S. Constitution:

> *No person shall be held to answer for a capital or otherwise infamous crime . . . nor shall any person be subject for the same offense to be twice put in jeopardy of life or limb; nor shall be compelled in any criminal case to be a witness against himself, nor be deprived of life, liberty, or property, without due process of law; nor shall private property be taken for public use without just compensation.*

These two amendments, part of the Bill of Rights, were written circa 1790. The Fifth was a reaction to British law of the time when lawyers could question suspects in such a way that they would incriminate themselves. The question "When did you stop beating your wife?" implies guilt. During the McCarthy hearings of the 1950s, innocent people—that is, ones loyal to their country and government—who had once belonged to the Communist Party had to invoke the Fifth Amendment to protect themselves from insidious questioning; yet, because they did so, they were blackballed. People assumed they were guilty of disloyalty as charged.

If you are accused of a crime and refuse to incriminate yourself by "taking the Fifth," you end up incriminating yourself anyway.

If you were on the witness stand accused of stealing, a skillful lawyer could make you seem guilty in the eyes of the jury even if you were innocent. It might behoove you, then, to refuse to testify. On the other hand, a hardened criminal can get away with years of crimes by invoking the Fifth Amendment. It is a dilemma worth examining from different levels of abstraction. If the level is high enough, as it currently is, the amendment protects everyone—you, me, and any criminal. If you go down a few rungs, you might recommend deleting this amendment so the criminals would go to jail. But then *you* would not be protected.

Name _____ Date _____

Truth Detectors (cont.)

Read each of the following slogans. By considering the degrees of generality and the class relationships of the terms, tear away the "concealing fabric" and get to your own truth. Write your considerations beneath each slogan.

1. *Use a Gun, Go to Jail*

_____

_____

_____

_____

2. *Power Corrupts: Absolute Power Corrupts Absolutely*

_____

_____

_____

_____

3. *Better Dead than Red*

_____

_____

_____

_____

4. *Peace with Honor*

_____

_____

_____

_____

Name _____ Date _____

Truth Detectors (cont.)

5. **Strength Through Joy**

_____

_____

6. **All We Have to Fear Is Fear Itself**

_____

_____

7. **Prosperity Is Just Around the Corner**

_____

_____

8. **Might Makes Right**

_____

_____

9. **Live Free or Die**

_____

_____

10. **Seeing Is Believing**

_____

_____

178

Name _____ Date _____

How Things Relate

Look at a political map of the world. Write the names of as many countries as there are students in the class on a piece of paper. Cut out each name, put them all in a bag, and draw one. The country you draw will be yours to explore.

Determine and describe the following information:

1. The size (land area) and population of your country:

   _____

2. The climate and geography as it varies from boundary to boundary:

   _____

   _____

   _____

3. The economy: What are its major exports, imports? What do most of the people do for a living?

   _____

   _____

   _____

   _____

4. The language, customs, and religions:

   _____

   _____

   _____

   _____

   _____

5. The eating habits of the people:

   _____

   _____

   _____

   _____

Name _____ Date _____

How Things Relate *(cont.)*

6. The stories of the country's wars—its history:

   _____

   _____

   _____

   _____

   _____

7. The major values of the people—what is important to them: Values are common to all countries but may be weighed differently. For example, people in the United States value freedom as well as security, but they talk often about liberty and rights. People from Russia are currently experiencing the strong pull of the value of authority against the value of individual freedom. People in China value wisdom of the ancients and obedience to elders. People in France value preservation of culture and art as well as freedom. Values do change, but slowly. Glean from your reading what the people of your country value most.

   _____

   _____

   _____

   _____

   _____

   _____

   _____

   _____

   _____

8. The major holidays of your country: How do people celebrate them?

   _____

   _____

   _____

   _____

   _____

Name _____ Date _____

How Things Relate *(cont.)*

9. The major plans for national defense: If your country were to go to war with another country, what would be your strategies for defense?

_____

_____

_____

_____

_____

_____

_____

_____

_____

_____

10. Draw a contour map of the country you are studying:

Name _____ Date _____

The Effects of Climate and Geography

In your group, compare countries. Ask questions about one another's countries. Add to your own information. Re-read all you have written about your country; then write a report that explains how the climate and geography of your country may be related to its wars, to its economy, to its food, to its values, and to its dealings with its neighbors.

_____
Name of Country

Relation of climate and geography to its wars:

_____

_____

Relation of climate and geography to its economy:

_____

_____

Relation of climate and geography to its food preferences:

_____

_____

Relation of climate and geography to its values:

_____

_____

Relation of climate and geography to dealings with its neighbors:

_____

_____

Name _____ Date _____

Conflict and War

On the map below, find your country and color it bright red.

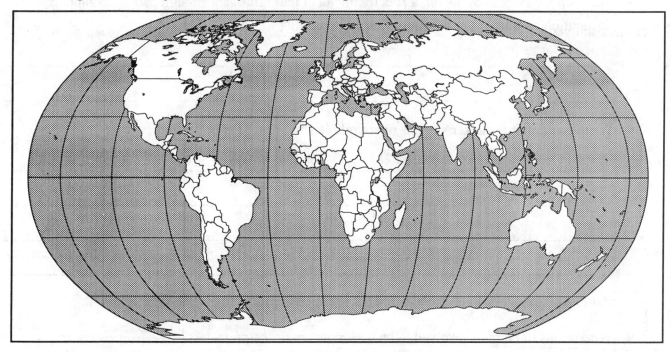

Now that you are quite familiar with your country, let's start a metaphorical world war. You will need to figure out who your allies would be and regroup accordingly.

◆ Your geographical neighbors might not be your allies. Consider Israel and Syria, for example.

◆ You might have religious allies. (If each country prays to God to win the war, how is God going to decide?)

◆ You might have trading partners with economic stakes in the war.

◆ You might have ideological partners, sharing similar social contracts.

◆ You might have dictators or kings who are relatives by blood or marriage.

◆ You might have a shared history and similar values, such as the United States and Great Britain.

Select your allies with care. Once you have regrouped accordingly, make a list of causes for this world war.

Causes

_____

_____

_____

_____

Name _____ Date _____

Conflict and War *(cont.)*

◆ Make up a precipitating factor, a specific incident that infuriates enough people to support a declaration of war:

_____

_____

◆ Write four bumper sticker slogans or sound bites to arouse the populace:

_____

_____

_____

_____

◆ Put under surveillance those citizens who take to the streets, opposing your war.

◆ Who seems to be most involved—the war mongers or the protesters?

_____

_____

◆ Decide on the type of war. Which weapons will be allowed? What will be the duration of the war?

_____

_____

◆ Return to your original group. Decide as a group who wins, based on all the written strategic defense plans.

_____

_____

◆ What are the consequences for the winners? What did it cost them to win? What did they profit?

_____

_____

Name _____ Date _____

Conflict and War *(cont.)*

◆ What are the consequences for the losers? What did it cost them? What did they profit?

_____

_____

◆ Picture yourself in the future, spending year after year in a dead-end job, bored with your wife or husband who is also in a dead-end job, bored with your friends and exhausted by your children, and feeling puny and insignificant. Is it possible you might then want your country to go to war?

◆ One thing about truth detectors—they can catch you when you are lying to yourself. In this last question on your world war, state how some persons might consider war to be fun.

_____

_____

How is war not fun at all? _____

_____

Is war ever worth the fun? _____

Abstractions and Concretions

The map is not the territory. A map, like numbers and words, is an abstraction and equally useful. Quickly create a map of your school and its grounds in the space below.

```
┌─────────────────────────────────────────────────┐
│                                                   │
│                                                   │
│                                                   │
│                                                   │
│                                                   │
│                                                   │
│                                                   │
└─────────────────────────────────────────────────┘
```

Compare your map with those of your classmates. Were they exactly alike? Anything alike? Imagine how explorers mapped previously undiscovered territories. How do you think they did it?

It is far easier to remember details of a map of territory you have entered than of territory you have never seen, felt, heard, or smelled. Why then, would we ever study world maps?

Compare your answers to these questions with others in your group.

Name _____ Date _____

Educated Guessing

A map is an abstraction, something the mind makes to represent a particular place. The following excerpts from literature are concrete descriptions of people and places throughout the world. From what you know about varying cultures and places, see how close you can come to guessing what area in the world each paragraph is describing. Discuss the readings in your group and make the best educated guesses you can. In the space below each paragraph, write the clues that led you to your guess. The first one is completed for you. Your teacher has the key for the rest.

The Avenida Pardo was still empty. Increasing his pace, he walked on till it crossed Avenida Grau; there he hesitated. He felt the cold—he had left his jacket in his room and his shirt alone was not enough to protect him from the wind which came from the sea and which combed the dense foliage of the rubber trees in a steady swish. The dreaded image of Flora and Ruben together gave him courage, and he went on walking. From the door of the bar beside the Montecarlo cinema, he saw them at their usual table, occupying the corner formed by the far and left-hand walls. Francisco, Melanes, Tobias. They noticed him and, after a second's surprise, they turned toward Ruben, their faces wicked and excited. He recovered himself at once—in front of men he certainly knew how to behave.

Continent: South America   **Country:** Peru

Clues: Spanish names, wind from the sea, dense foliage of rubber trees. "In front of men he certainly knew how to behave."

(If you don't know the continent, name the area, such as "Mideast" for Turkey, Israel, etc.)

1. *I went to my mother's hut and sat there. I was wearing lots of beads and my hair was completely covered and full with ornaments.*

   That night there was another dance. We danced, and some people fell asleep and others kept dancing. In the early morning, Tashay and his relatives went back to their camp; we went into our huts to sleep. When morning was late in the sky, they came back. They stayed around and then his parents said, "Because we are only staying a short while—tomorrow, let's start building the marriage hut."

   Continent/Area: _____ **Country:** _____

   Clues: _____

   _____

   _____

   _____

   _____

   _____

186

Name _____ Date _____

Educated Guessing (cont.)

2. *When I woke up, I stared down at my feet in the black mountain dirt. Little black ants were swarming over the pine needles around my foot. They must have smelled the apricots. I thought about my family far below me. They would be wondering about me, because this had never happened to me before. The tribal police would file a report. But if old Grandpa weren't dead he would tell them what happened—he would laugh and say, "Stolen by a ka'tsina, a mountain spirit. She'll come home—they usually do."*

   Continent/Area: _____ **Country:** _____

   Clues:_____

   _____

   _____

3. *First, one of the young men who had been fighting earlier with a long pole performed the "Drunken Sword." In this style the fighter must stumble, weave, leap and bob as if drunk, at the same time whipping his sword around him at full speed, all the while maintaining perfect control. Then a woman with a single braid reaching to her waist performed the double saber. The two blades flashed around her but never touched, and she finished by leaping into the air, crossing the sabers, and landing in a full split.*

   Continent/Area: _____ **Country:** _____

   Clues:_____

   _____

   _____

4. *We'd heard Hasani yelling. My ma had sworn at Hasani's dad. She said, "Why are you beating an innocent child?" I saw the marks the belt had left on his shoulders, and a place under one eye that had gotten swollen and turned black and blue. Every night when Hasani's dad came home, before he changed clothes or washed, he would beat Hasani. He would beat him with his fists. He'd kick him. He'd use a club, or a rope, or a belt. He swore at Hasani and beat him till he cried bloody murder; you could hear him scream all over the place.*

   The neighbors would go running up. They'd swear, "May I die and you die," and make him let him go. Hasani's dad would beat him every night, but my dad would only beat Ahmad and me once or twice a week.

   Continent/Area: _____ **Country:** _____

   Clues:_____

   _____

   _____

Name _____ Date _____

Educated Guessing (cont.)

5. *The New Year's right after Fred had moved out, I remember walking Evelyn home from the Laughorne's up Salem Street just before morning, an inch of new snow on the sidewalk and everything silent except for her voice, going on and on about Fred. There had been Stingers, and she could hardly walk, and I wasn't much better. The housefronts along Salem calm as ghosts, and the new snow like mica reflecting the streetlights. We climbed her porch steps, and that living room, with its wide floorboards, her tree still up, and a pine wreath hung on an oak peg in the fireplace lintel, hit me as if we had walked smack into an old-fashioned children's book.*

Continent/Area: _____ **Country:** _____

Clues: _____

6. *At our house this has been a day of great uneasiness. After several hours, the girl emerged. She was wearing a sari, maybe for the first time. She stepped out on the veranda, straightening her sari and carrying a coconut. Her swaying walk was restricted considerably by the sari and she moved forward with an eye on each step. She hadn't veiled herself in any way, nor, with her husband walking so close to her, did she show any of the embarrassment and coquettishness of a traditional bride.*

The Father made a pronouncement—"In the old days, girls would cry all the way to the edge of the village. Anyone who didn't was beaten and forced to cry. Otherwise her life at her husband's home could never be happy. The old days are passing and men's hearts have become machines, just machines!" At such times his voice grows sharp, and the wreckage of Kali Yug, this Age of Darkness, dances before his eyes.

Continent/Area: _____ **Country:** _____

Clues: _____

_____

7. *If I lay across the lawn before our house, face upwards to the sky, my head towards the Bishops Court, each spread-out leg would point to the inner compounds of Lower Parsonage. Half of the Anglican Girl's School occupied one of these lower spaces, the other half had taken over Bishops Court. The lower area contained the school's junior classrooms, a dormitory, a small fruit garden of pawpaws, guava, some bamboo, and wild undergrowth. There were always snails to be found in the rainy season. In the other lower compound was the mission bookseller, a shriveled man with a serene wife on whose ample back we all, at one time or the other slept, or reviewed the world. His compound became a short cut to the road that led to Ibara, Lafenwa, or Igbein and its Grammar School over which Ransome-Kuti presided and lived with his family. The bookseller's compound contained the only well in the parsonage; in the dry season, his place was never empty. And his soil appeared to produce the only coconut trees.*

Continent/Area: _____ **Country:** _____

Clues: _____

_____

Name _____ Date _____

Educated Guessing *(cont.)*

8. *"What can you do as a simple laborer?"*

    "Quite a bit. First of all, after I lay tiles in the bathroom or kitchen of an Israeli settler, when the tiles are all in place and the cement has already dried, I take a hammer and break a few. When we finish installing sewage pipes, and the Jewish subcontractor has checked to see that everything is all right, then I stuff a sackful of cement into the pipe. As soon as water runs through that pipe the cement gets hard as a rock, and the sewage system becomes blocked."

    Continent/Area: _____ **Country:** _____

    Clues: _____

    _____

    _____

9. *I begin to suspect that the intensity with which the children contemplate the idea of good and evil residing in the same person has some connection with their unorthodox views of revenge as charity. That morning one of the other children I spoke with, Gnem Thy Pak, a boy of sixteen, told of watching a Khmer Rouge soldier cut a man's throat in the jungle. When I asked what it is that makes someone do so dreadful a thing, he, like the other children, responded that some people are born with a good spirit inside them, some with a bad one, and that these two warring spirits cannot coexist in the same person.*

    Continent/Area: _____ **Country:** _____

    Clues: _____

    _____

    _____

10. *Playing hooky from work is a national pastime so common that Arkady Raikin, the comedian, has gotten censors to approve several skits on that theme. In one, he plays an engineer who lolls all day on a bed the size of a putting green and rationalizes skipping work by recalling how little he does on the job. "I'm doing them a favor by staying away," he quips. In another, three men sneak out during working hours to the barbershop but get lousy service because the barbers themselves are trying to sneak away. One barber wants to buy oranges, another, to get some gadget repaired, and the third to visit the dentist. The barbers return defeated, only to discover that the grocer, repairman, and dentist are the three customers sitting in their chairs.*

    Continent/Area: _____ **Country:** _____

    Clues: _____

    _____

    _____

Name _____Date _____

Educated Guessing *(cont.)*

11. *Down in the villages of the Chukurova plain, a sure sign of oncoming spring is when the women are seen with their heads on one another's lap, picking the lice out of one another's hair. So it was, on one of the first warm days of the year. A balmy sun shone caressingly down on the fields and village, and not a leaf stirred. A group of women were sitting before their huts on the dusty ground, busy with the lice and wagging their tongues for all they were worth. An acrid odor of sweat hung about the group. Seedy Doneh was rummaging in the hair of a large woman who was stretched full length on the ground. She decided that she had been silent long enough.*

    Continent/Area: _____ **Country:** _____

    Clues:_____

    _____

    _____

    _____

    _____

    _____

12. *Traditional American cooking is a cuisine without mystery: simple, nourishing, scantily seasoned foods. No tricks: a carrot is a homely, honest carrot, a potato is not ashamed of its humble condition, and a steak is a big, bloody hunk of meat. This is a transubstantiation of the democratic virtues of the Founding Fathers; a plain meal, one dish following another like the sensible, unaffected sentences of a virtuous discourse. Like the conversation among those at table, the relation between substances and flavors is direct: sauces that make tastes, garnishes that entice the eye, condiments that confuse the taste buds are taboo. The separation of one food from another is analogous to the reserve that characterizes the relations between sexes, races, and classes. In our country food is a communion, not only between those together at table but between ingredients; Yankee food, impregnated with Puritanism, is based on exclusions. The maniacal preoccupation with the purity and origin of food products has its counterpart in racism and exclusivism. In the Yankee culinary tradition our fondness for dark, passionate stews such as moles, for thick and sumptuous red, green and yellow sauces, would be scandalous.*

    Continent/Area: _____ **Country:** _____

    Clues:_____

    _____

    _____

    _____

    _____

    _____

190

Name _____ Date _____

Educated Guessing (cont.)

13. *What I saw in Elvis Presley, beyond sheer physical gorgeousness, was the possibility of the impossible. The upper lip, the sneer were a direct extension of the Teddy Boys and Roseland. For Elvis, I sensed at once and soon discovered for a fact, was derived from the same unregarded stable. He too had started out foredoomed, dispossessed, the most hopeless of White Trash. His ambition had been to grow up into a truck driver. He'd envied their freedom. But such heroics, he understood, were beyond him. In the crunch, he was too soft-skinned, too scared, too much a mother's boy. A true trucker he could never be. So he became a Messiah instead.*

    All rock shows, artifacts, and films were outlawed. And anyone who challenged this suppression was in for a bumpy ride. Mary Fadden, a comely fifth-former at Northlands, the local girl's school, was expelled for secreting a picture of Jerry Lee Lewis in her desk; discs and posters fueled bonfires; and Elvis himself was ceremonially torched in effigy at the Brandywell Football Grounds, nailed to a flaming cross.

    Continent/Area: _____ **Country:** _____

    Clues: _____

    _____

    _____

    _____

14. *The man who had uncovered the coins stared at me long and hard. As the others drifted out onto the street, this man shoved his rice aside, leaned over me, and asked if I would be so kind as to accompany him to meet his family. Something urgent in his voice intrigued me; I nodded. Outside, he turned off to the right before reaching the sand, and I followed him through the rice paddies, balancing like a tightrope-walker on one of the dikes that separate the flooded squares. To our left the village spread itself out along the shore: A young woman nursed an infant, smoke rose from cooking fires, three pigs rummaged through a pile of rags and wood.*

    At his home, the man gripped my ankle and began to explain his situation. Essentially what he had to say was this: that he was a poor and ignorant fisherman blessed with a loving wife and many children, and that despite his steady and enthusiastic propitiation of the local gods and ancestors, he had been unable to catch any fish for the last six months. This was especially upsetting since before that time he had been one of the most successful fishermen in the village. He said it was evident to everyone in the village that his present difficulties were the result of some left-handed magic; clearly a demon had been induced by some sorcery to take up residence in the hull of his fishing boat.

    Continent/Area: _____ **Country:** _____

    Clues: _____

    _____

    _____

    _____

The Game of Politics

1. Brainstorm several current political issues—world, country, city, school—and list them on the board.

2. In preparation for partner interviews, read the following hypothetical interviews as models.

Question: Are you in favor of gun control?

Answer: *Of course.*

> **Q.** *Does this include BB guns, water pistols, and arcade computer simulations?*
> **A.** *Well, not water pistols or arcade games. They're harmless.*
> **Q.** *How about guns used in movies?*
> **A.** *No. That's storytelling. The guns don't actually kill anyone.*
> **Q.** *How close is storytelling, imagination, to action?*
> **A.** *I don't know.*
> **Q.** *Are you still in favor of gun control?*
> **A.** *Well, yes.*
> **Q.** *Then where do you draw the line? How would you draw the line?*

Question: *Should women have the same rights as men?*

Answer: *Sure.*

> **Q.** *And the same responsibilities?*
> **A.** *Well, sure—if they can make the same money.*
> **Q.** *How can women give birth and still have the energy to make the same money?*
> **A.** *Well, they could if the men helped out.*
> **Q.** *Helped out how?*
> **A.** *With diapers and all.*
> **Q.** *That's only part of the equation. What about the women whose children are grown or who don't have children at all?*
> **A.** *They have the same rights as men.*
> **Q.** *How come they don't think so?*
> **A.** *Because they can't make the same money, and they don't have the physical strength.*
> **Q.** *Then you don't think they should have the same rights and responsibilities?*
> **A.** *Well, they shouldn't have to go to war.*
> **Q.** *What if they want to?*
> **A.** *Then they should get equal pay.*

3. Choose a partner, an issue for an interview, and take turns conducting interviews in which you question each answer until you are satisfied you cannot delve any deeper.

4. Return to your groups and, as a class, carefully choose the issue you wish to debate. Decide which groups will be on which sides of the issue. Choose a moderator to keep discussions on task and reasonable.

5. Choose a group spokesperson to debate with other groups' representatives in front of the class.

6. Begin debate. After ten minutes, regroup for new strategies.

7. Continue debate. Regroup if necessary.

Name _____ Date _____

Sandwich Critique

On the lines below, write a "sandwich" critique of the debate with the two "slices of bread" being the parts that were well debated and the "meat" being the part that could use some improvement. Make note of problems with or successes at recognizing varying levels of abstraction.

Compare one another's critiques; then file them in your portfolios.

I was first impressed with the following strong points:

_____

_____

_____

_____

_____

_____

_____

It seems to me that the following elements of the debate could be improved:

_____

_____

_____

_____

_____

_____

_____

Finally, I would like to emphasize what I think were the best parts of the debate:

_____

_____

_____

_____

_____

_____

Name _____ Date _____

Social Contracts

People need to cooperate to survive. They need to play together to enjoy survival. To that end, groups of people have formed social contracts with each other, contracts that attempt to spell out mutually agreed upon rules of conduct. As groups of people grow to fill the boundaries of a large continent such as Australia or North America, the social contracts become more complex and require the ongoing examination of a supreme court.

What are the social contracts of your classroom—not just those imposed on you by rules of the teacher and administration, but those you and your classmates chose and abide by?

_____

_____

_____

_____

When a given social contract grows, its growth, like that of a puppy, is determined by its genetics. In the case of a social contract, the prevailing wisdom at the time of its inception directs its growth over centuries. For example, the Protestant Reformation of the 15th Century brought forth the idea of individual salvation and individual liberty. When everyone is responsible for his/her own salvation, one sees one's role in society as equal to others. This spurs the onset of democracy. One no longer looks to authority figures to lead one.

Democracy is a hard-won social contract because it takes so much work. Sometimes it is easier to let a dictator make all the decisions. Once we let a dictator take over, unless we happen to be his favored friends, we are apt to suffer. When things are going well, we slack off, let down our guards, and soon a leopard pounces. If our democratic infrastructure is strong, we can fend off the attack and survive the pounce.

When the disparity between the haves and the have-nots becomes too great, the have-nots often start a revolution. Subsequent social contracts depend on the intellectual climate of the time. The French revolution occurred during the "Enlightenment," a period of intellectual soul searching about social contracts, and long before Karl Marx published his philosophy for the ultimate social contract— communal ownership of everything. Therefore, subsequent social contracts in France support individual liberty and a capitalistic economy. In Russia, however, the overthrow of the Czar by the people occurred after Karl Marx. It made sense to the Russians to try communism. And it might have worked if human nature had not interfered.

How did human nature interfere?

_____

_____

_____

Name _____ Date _____

Social Contracts *(cont.)*

Take another look at a political map of the world. Divide the world into Western Europe, Great Britain and all English-speaking countries, The Orient, Africa, Middle East, Eastern Europe, and South America. Choose one of these large sections and look up the history of their social contracts. For example, in the Middle East you would look up two or three countries such as Turkey, Iran, and Saudi Arabia. What do their social contracts, their forms of government, have in common?

Each person in your group should be responsible for reporting on at least one country's history of governing. When you have gathered enough information, speculate on the historical causes of the current social contract in your section of the world. Write a paragraph of your speculations, ending with your prediction for future contracts.

_____

_____

_____

_____

_____

◆ ◆ ◆ ◆

Political Role Play

Write the following terms on separate scraps of paper:

Republic-Democratic   **Republic-Dictator**

Anarchy

Democratic-Socialism   **Monarchy-Empire**

In your group, draw from a hat one of the above forms of government. Prepare to argue your case for that form of government. Define your form on several levels of abstraction. Create a mythical country.

Name and Brief Description: _____

_____

_____

Size of Population: _____

_____

_____

Take turns arguing for your form of government. As a group, decide who presented the best argument. Each group then sends its most persuasive speaker to debate in front of the class. As a class, discuss the criteria you used to decide who was the best in your group.

Family History

The stories of history that you hear and read are not all of history, just the most interesting—the highlights, so to speak. It would take more than a normal lifetime to read the complete history of a given nation or tribe.

Obviously, some editors in the past have selected those events to be recorded as a given history. Imagine what they did not include.

Family histories work the same way. We write of the "significant" events in the family's life, the occasional successes, and the births, marriages, and deaths.

Sometimes we read about family feuds. "Aunt Jenny didn't speak to Aunt Lizzie for 45 years. Neither one could remember why." More often, those stories are left out.

The history of a family, tribe, or nation shapes its future. What each of us does or does not do today affects that future. For example, if you live in a democratic republic and do not vote, you give up your power to the ones who do vote. If your family decides to move to a different country, it affects the future of the family in a most dramatic way. If your country invades another country with the aim of taking land, its future is profoundly affected. If it wins, it becomes vulnerable to retaliation. If it loses, it loses pride as well as economic advantage.

A civil war is a family feud intensified. The reverberations last for centuries.

When you tossed a pebble into the water, you could see the ripples grow in size and number. Think now, metaphorically, of a time you or someone you knew threw the proverbial pebble into the water. You did something that at the time seemed insignificant, but the ripples are still growing. For example, when I was 10 years old I went to town with two friends on Halloween and decided to ring the church bell. I climbed up into the belfry. My two friends saw the police coming and ran away. I was ringing the bell so didn't hear them. When I climbed down and saw the police car, I ran too. I managed to get away without being caught, but I felt so guilty for my actions I could tell no one. For years I was frightened, sure I would be punished for such blasphemy. I had nightmares about it. When that bell rang, the ripples in the air did not stop for 10 years.

On the other hand, one time I decided to learn how to save people who were drowning. (Most likely, I wanted the badge for successfully completing the course.) Then one day I was swimming in a lake with a friend who suffered a bad cramp in her leg. She panicked and went under. I knew how to contain her panic and swim her to shore, which I did. Pretty good ripples!

We do not know how our daily decisions affect our futures, but we can look at histories and get an inkling. Look again at what you wrote about the country you drew out of the bag. Think about its future. What in its past will shape its future?

Now think about your own family's history. Go way back, if you can.

196

Name _____ Date _____

Family History *(cont.)*

1. Quickwrite your family's history here. Include your family's values and general attitudes toward life. (Quickwrite means just that. Do not worry about organization or grammar at this point.)

_____

_____

_____

_____

_____

_____

_____

_____

_____

_____

_____

_____

2. If possible, read your quickwrite to your grandparents or a family friend. Find the oldest people in your family. Interview them. Ask for more information. From what they will tell you, what would you include? What would you leave out? Are there conflicting stories?

3. Rewrite your family history. Organize it according to generalities with supporting specifics.

4. Do a read-around in your group where each member reads everyone else's history.

5. Clear up any confusion your readers point out. Add. Explain.

6. Write a prediction based on your family's history. Where will your family be 10 years from now, and what will they be doing? Twenty years from now? Thirty years from now?

7. Congratulate one another and fill your portfolios.

Name _____ Date _____

Shared Culture: The News

One facet of the social contract is a shared culture. As in family-speak (members of the same family using shortcuts and abbreviations or just looks to communicate to each other) members of a shared culture and history understand what other members mean by what they write, say, or broadcast on television.

In your group, decide on a specific period of time and a specific country for your created television news broadcast. Assign one another tasks such as researcher, news writers, prompter, and anchors, and help one another put on a credible news broadcast for the rest of the class. Your audience (the class) will have to guess the time and place of your broadcast.

For example, suppose these words to be the opening sound bites: *"The streets are swarming with civilians, men and women alike, piling old furniture to form barricades. Uniformed soldiers are being outrun by the unruly mob."* If you were to add details such as horses and carriages, royalty, and guillotines, your audience would know immediately that it was the French Revolution.

To prepare for your broadcast, decide on your country, period, and event; then research answers to the following questions. (Add more questions as you think of them.)

1. What basic ways of living did the people who could watch your news program share?

   _____

   _____

   _____

   _____

2. What business or government would sponsor your show? What would the commercials advertise?

   _____

   _____

   _____

   _____

3. What are the divisive issues of the time and place?

   _____

   _____

   _____

   _____

4. What is the common religion, if any?

   _____

Name _____ Date _____

Shared Culture: The News (cont.)

5. What recent events led to the current situation?

_____

_____

_____

6. What historical events led to the current situation?

_____

_____

_____

7. What is the scientific and technological news of the time?

_____

_____

_____

8. Who are the influential philosophers? (They need not be current with your time period but widely read during your time period. For example, Aristotle advocated limited democracy and mutual tolerance, among many other ideas, but heartily disapproved of charging interest on borrowed money. Saint Augustine, in the fourth century, excused slavery, called it moral, and advocated obedience to a master or sovereign even if he were evil.)

_____

_____

_____

_____

9. What form of government is in power?

_____

_____

_____

10. What are the most popular forms of entertainment?

_____

_____

_____

Culture, History, and Growth

Finally, one more reading follows of William James' exuberant paragraph from "Will to Believe":

> *Man's chief difference from the brutes lies in the exuberant excess of his subjective propensities. His preeminence over them lies simply and solely in the number and in the fantastic and unnecessary character of his wants, physical, moral, aesthetic and intellectual. Had his whole life not been a quest for the superfluous, he would never have established himself so inexpungeably in the necessary. And from the consciousness of this, he should draw the lesson that his wants are to be trusted, that even when their gratification seems furthest off, the uneasiness they occasion is still the best guide of his life, and will lead him to issues entirely beyond his present powers of reckoning. Prune down his extravagances, sober him, and you undo him.*

All human beings are both brutes and angels, brilliant at times and stupid at other times, jealous and vengeful, secure and forgiving, petty and mean, kind and honorable. Our belief systems direct our actions. Our actions have consequences—from the ridiculous to the sublime—with a few wars in between.

◆ Wars continue to baffle, entertain, and devastate us.

◆ All we can do is learn to grow from our personal experience—and from social studies, a subject that cannot be separated from any other subject. It permeates them all.

◆ The history of science and technology directs the future of science and technology.

◆ The history of mathematics points out its future—the ultimate abstraction.

◆ The history of literature is the story of people—the part that makes us angels when we let it.

◆ The history of art is like that of language. It links us from generation to generation, from country to country. Michelangelo and Picasso are comrades in arms.

◆ The history of the world, like our own personal histories, is made up of fascinating stories, tragedies and comedies, comedy-tragedy.

And the ladder of abstraction reaches beyond our galaxy, beckoning us to stretch our understanding farther and farther into the universe.

Name _____ Date _____

Final Essay

On the lines below, write your answer to this question:

Are social systems progressing or simply recycling?

Think about it, discuss it in your group, and then write your answer. Support your opinion with at least five concrete examples. (Remember, there is no right answer to this questions, simply well reasoned and supported ones.) Critique it according to the scoring guide below, rewrite it on separate paper if necessary, and turn it in for your portfolio.

_____

Essay Title

_____

_____

_____

_____

_____

_____

_____

_____

_____

_____

_____

Scoring Guide

1. The writer opens with a clear statement of opinion directly related to the question.

2. The writer supports his opinion with three specific examples.

3. The writer supports his opinion with five specific examples.

4. The writer follows standard conventions of written expression.

All 4 = A, 3 = B, 2 = C, 1 = D

Answer Key

Abstraction

Since the idea is to foster problem solving through the perception of relationships, answers can and should vary. Below are suggested answers.

Page 11

Ant and oak tree are both alive.

Page 12

Below

Page 14

(Example of each kind of analysis)

Classification: Flowers

Structure: Sailboat

Operation: Wedding

Page 16

(Suggested diagram)

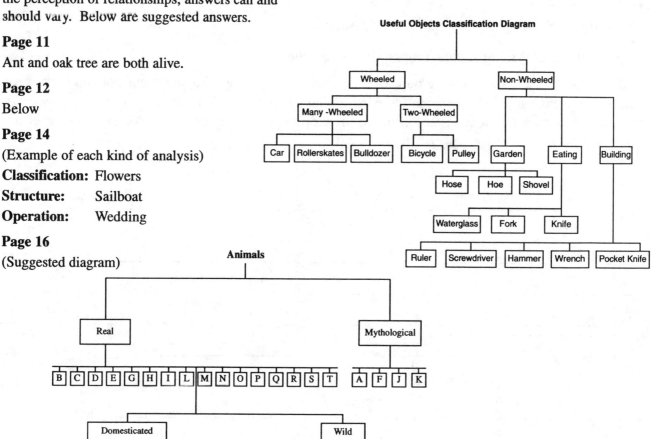

Page 18

(Suggested diagram)

Page 19

One of many ways these items could be classified:

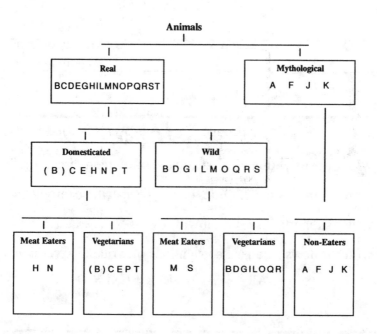

Answer Key *(cont.)*

Abstraction *(cont.)*

Page 21
Possible sorting factors:

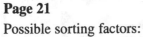

Page 25

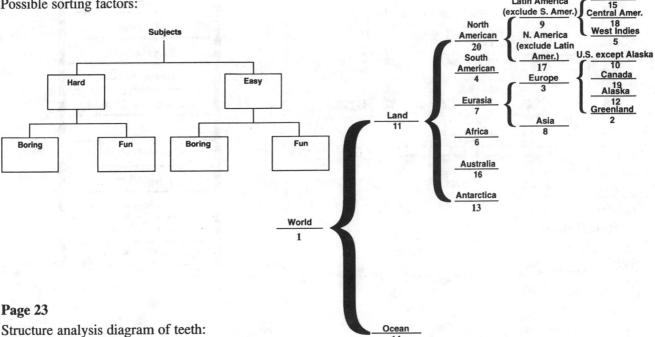

Page 23
Structure analysis diagram of teeth:

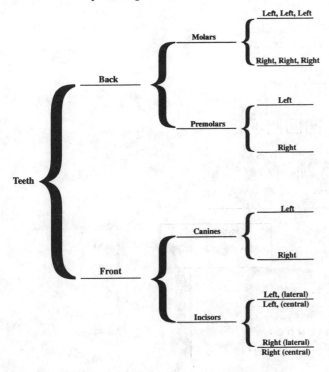

Page 28
I. Earth to Mercury
    A. Earth to Vicinity of Venus
        1. Earth to Moon
        2. Moon to Vicinity of Venus
    B. Vicinity of Venus to Mercury
II. Mercury to Mars
    A. Mercury to Vicinity of Venus
    B. Vicinity of Venus to Vicinity of Earth
    C. Vicinity of Earth to Mars
III. Mars to Earth

Page 29
I. Prepare Invitations (7)
    A. Set Date & Time (6)
    B. Send Invitations (3)
II. Arrange Entertainment (1)
    A. Plan Games (10)
    B. Gather Prizes (5)
III. Decide on Necessary Supplies (4)
    A. Make Grocery List (9)
    B. Buy Groceries (8)
    C. Bake Cake (2)

Answer Key *(cont.)*

Science

Page 44

- Science (5)
  - Earth (4)
    - Oceanography (2)
    - Astronomy (7)
    - Meteorology (11)
    - Geology (17)
  - Physical (15)
    - Matter (18)
      - Solids (6)
      - Gases (13)
      - Liquids (9)
    - Energy (14)
      - Kinetic (16)
      - Potential (1)
  - Life (9)
    - Cell (12)
      - Plants (10)
      - Animals (3)

Page 46
Scientific Process

I. Observe
- A. Qualitative
  1. Identify
  2. Describe
- B. Quantitative
  1. Metric
  2. Meniscus
  3. Chart Occurrences

II. Analyze
- A. Relationship to Others
- B. Structure

III. Synthesize
- A. Hypothesize
- B. Describe Theory

IV. Test

Page 48

Matter
Element
Periodic Table
Atomic Number
Atomic Mass Number
Atom
Nucleus
Electrons
Shells
Protons & Neutrons
Quarks

Page 49

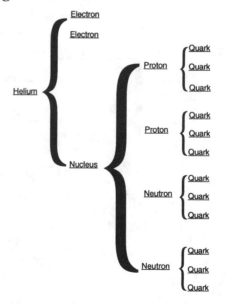

Answer Key *(cont.)*

Page 55

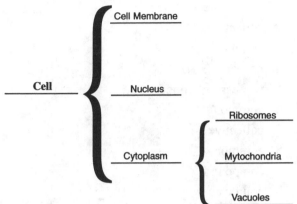

1. prefix "de"
2. ribo
3. oxy for oxygen
4. nucleic

Page 59

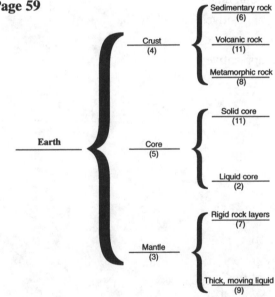

Language

Pages 71–72

(Suggested Similitudes)

Visual: snowy for hair, mouse for computer control, delta for river sediment fan

Affective: muck, sweetheart, dude

Logical: lemon for car, cell for housing a nucleus or a prisoner, glass ceiling for invisible upper limits of promotion

Ironies: calling an old man "youngster"; a tall person, "shorty"; a black eye, a "beauty"

Pages 73–75

1. Genus-species: specialization
2. Operational: operation to phase
3. Structural: whole-to-part
4. Operational: Phase to operation
5. Genus-species: specialization
6. Sensory-similitude: auditory
7. Abstract-concrete: concretion
8. Genus-species: generalization
9. Irony
10. Sensory-similitude: affective
11. Sensory-similitude: visual
12. Sensory-similitude: logical
13. Abstract-concrete: concretion
14. Structural: part-to-whole

Pages 77–78

1. clothes
2. plant
3. mood
4. virtue
5. mountain
6. birth
7. fish
8. mouth
9. size
10. farmer
11. sun
12. alphabet
13. swan

Language *(cont.)*

Pages 79–80

(Sample metaphorical uses)

Heart: Heart of the matter, the program, the story

Cut: Cut to the chase, cut up, cut across the street

Wing: Let's wing it, on the wing, broken wing

Dead: Engine's dead, dead wrong, dead center

Right: Right on, civil right, cut right to the heart of the matter

Page 81

Why would I say that without language you can't have pizza?

Suggested response: You have to think of a "pie" and consider variations. Think "cheese and meat toppings" as variations; borrow word from Italian. Think bread crust, oven.

Pages 83–84

1. Metaphor
2. Both
3. Metaphor
4. Suggestion: You are so witty you've given a wild new meaning to the word.
5. A person's life
6. Words have dominion over the world. Mankind uses words.
7. Yes
8. Words from an egotist who acts superior to others
9. Simile
10. Poetry and fiction resemble the real world of time and space. The worlds they create on paper are no stronger than a flower; yet, the ideas they suggest are eternal and indestructible.
11. Wise men use words as tools for thought; fools spill them recklessly.

Page 86

1. compound
2. collective
3. common
4. proper
5. possessive pronoun
6. common
7. collective
8. common
9. compound
10. noun clause
11. common
12. proper
13. common
14. pronoun
15. noun clause
16. appositive
17. possessive pronoun
18. appositive

Answer Key *(cont.)*

Language *(cont.)*

Page 88

Verb Forms

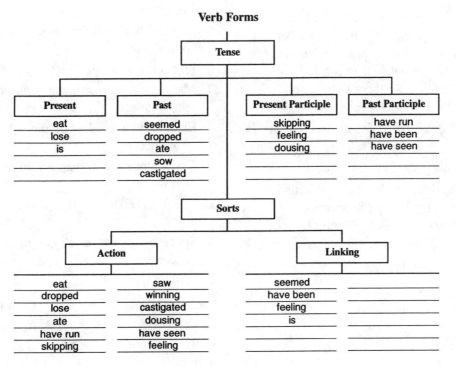

Page 89

1. gerund
2. participle as adjective
3. intransitive
4. transitive
5. present perfect
6. past perfect
7. present participle
8. infinitive
9. linking
10. intransitive
11. helping
12. past perfect progressive

Page 96

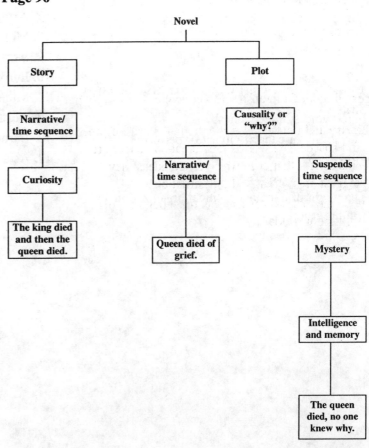

Answer Key (cont.)

Mathematics

Page 162: Game for forming concepts. Students who analyze the given information will choose Heather, Joe, Duke, and Maria to solve the problem because they understand the use of statistics to confuse, the prevalence of pseudo-scientific theories based on illogical use of numbers, and the need for clear, logical thought in problem solving.

Page 164: Money is an abstraction, a system of symbols that varies from country to country but is used the same way at the same level of abstraction. Amount of money will not change its level of abstraction, only its buying power—which is another abstraction.

End of Section Test, page 171
Part I
No, it is not a reasonable claim.
Part II
1. joke
2. yoke
3. albumen
4. 50
5. not enough information
6. yolk

Social Studies

Page 175
Suggested order from abstract to concrete:
7. Forcefulness; effectiveness
1. The ability or capacity to act or perform effectively
3. Strength or force exerted: might
6. The might of a nation, political organization, or similar group
5. A person, group or nation having great influence over others
4. The ability or official capacity to exercise control: authority
8. Physics: the rate at which work is done…
10. Mathematics: a. exponent b. number of elements in a finite set
9. Electricity: a. product of applied potential difference…
11. Optics: measure of magnification of optical instrument…
12. Theology: sixth group of angels in hierarchical order…
2. Specific capacity, faculty, or aptitude: power of concentration

Pages 186–191

Continent/Area	Country
1. Africa	Botswana
2. North America	U.S.
3. Asia	China
4. Mideast	Iran
5. North America	U.S.
6. Asia	India
7. Africa	Nigeria
8. Mideast	Palestine
9. Asia	Cambodia
10. Europe	Russia
11. Mideast	Turkey
12. North America	Mexico
13. Europe	Ireland
14. Asia	Bali